PROTECTING TRADE SECRETS UNDER THE UNIFORM TRADE SECRETS ACT

PROTECTING TRADE SECRETS UNDER THE UNIFORM TRADE SECRETS ACT

Practical Advice for Executives

Michael Craig Budden

Q

QUORUM BOOKS
Westport, Connecticut • London

Library of Congress Cataloging-in-Publication Data

Budden, Michael Craig.
Protecting trade secrets under the Uniform Trade Secrets Act :
practical advice for executives / Michael Craig Budden.
p.   cm.
Includes bibliographical references and indexes.
ISBN 1–56720–016–8 (alk. paper)
1. Trade secrets—United States—States. I. Title.
KF3197.B83   1996
346.7304'8—dc20   96–3622
[347.30648]

British Library Cataloguing in Publication Data is available.

Library of Congress Catalog Card Number: 96–3622
ISBN: 1–56720–016–8

First published in 1996

Quorum Books, 88 Post Road West, Westport, CT 06881
An imprint of Greenwood Publishing Group, Inc.

Printed in the United States of America

The paper used in this book complies with the
Permanent Paper Standard issued by the National
Information Standards Organization (Z39.48–1984).

10 9 8 7 6 5 4 3 2 1

This book is dedicated to

Connie, Heather, and Staci

Contents

Preface

Firms possess valuable information that gives them competitive advantages. Such information is sometimes referred to as "trade secrets." A trade secret can be something as simple as a pizza sauce recipe or as complicated as a recipe for making synthetic diamonds. Incidents of theft or misappropriation of trade secrets continue at an alarming rate. The cost to businesses totals in the billions of dollars annually. Trade secrets theft is on the rise.

Executives need to recognize which information they possess that can qualify as a trade secret and take proactive steps to protect that information. A plan of action that can provide reasonably for the continued maintenance of secrecy needs to be implemented and monitored. The plan needs to take into account the provisions of the Uniform Trade Secrets Act (UTSA).

The UTSA is a state law that, since its debut in 1979, has been enacted in 40 states and the District of Columbia. It is likely to be adopted by the remaining states soon. The UTSA offers executives protection for their trade secrets and remedies should they find themselves victim to a trade secrets misappropriation. Executives desiring to avail themselves of the UTSA need to recognize the existence of trade secrets in their firms, provide for their security, and monitor their firms' efforts aimed at maintaining their secrecy. A plan of action with the purpose of improving one's strategic efforts to protect trade secrets under the provisions of the UTSA is presented. Executives should take proactive steps to protect their firms' secrets and assure the continued success of their firms' competitive efforts. As is emphasized in the text, the importance of securing competent legal counsel, given that trade secrets protection involves the law, is of paramount importance.

The steps in the plan are paired with summaries of legal cases concerning various questions related to trade secrets that serve to explain the importance of each step. For those desiring a more in-depth discussion, full case discussions are available in West Publishing Company's *Reporter* series, available in law libraries and many university and public libraries possessing legal collections. The author acknowledges the importance to understanding trade secrets law as contained in cases available in the *Reporter*, published by West Publishing, St. Paul, Minnesota, and encourages those desiring more information to seek such information in the *Reporter*s, because summaries included in this text are, necessarily, brief.

Acknowledgments

The author acknowledges materials contributed by Renée D. Culverhouse and John W. Yeargain in the form of restrictive covenants they prepared for inclusion in Chapter 3. Thanks, too, to the National Conference of Commissioners on Uniform State Laws, which gave permission to include the Uniform Trade Secrets Act in Chapter 2. In addition, the author acknowledges the contribution that Robert C. Lake played in assisting the author to recognize the role the act played in strategic business planning. Finally, the author would like to thank his parents, Rowland and Wava Budden, for instilling in their children an appreciation for education.

1

Introduction to Trade Secrets

What a bad month. Thinking back, you realize that it all started to go wrong a few weeks ago. You were home watching television, and a competitor's advertising came on during one of your favorite shows. You recognized the creative scenario and the jingle incorporated into the advertisement as being very similar to a series of promotions your marketing department had been preparing for your firm. Your firm's advertisements were scheduled to begin airing next month. A substantial investment in the planned advertising campaign appeared to be wasted, and your hopes for a successful marketing effort began to sink. The creative process would have to begin again. New print and broadcast advertising undoubtedly would have to be developed. New point-of-purchase displays would have to be designed. Redoing all of these tasks would take time to do well. The delay would impact several competitive moves that your firm had planned to initiate. The bottom line would take a hit. That evening, you went to bed with a headache.

Things worsened. A few days later, the director of your real estate department called and bemoaned the fact that a prime location that had been chosen to anchor your next major expansion had just been optioned by a competitor. The competitor had beaten your real estate department to the punch. You recognized what surely was an odd coincidence, in that the competitor that optioned the property is the same competitor that had preempted your advertising program. What a coup for them. They managed to preempt your competitive efforts twice in one week. Your firm's major investment in the location research that resulted in the hoped-for location has been for naught. Additional research will be necessary, and a potentially less desirable location will have to be chosen for your firm's new location. The thought of the delay involved and the possibility that a location with less than maximum site characteristics would have to be chosen to anchor your new office makes you reach for the antacid bottle.

It didn't seem to get any better the next week. Late one afternoon, you discovered that your computer processing system, which allowed for a significant increase in processing speed and capacity for handling your firm's inventory and purchasing transactions and which took more than 18 months for your staff to design and develop, apparently has been duplicated by a competitor. The system was giving your firm a competitive edge in maintaining needed inventory on a just-in-time basis, had improved your firm's ability to service customers, and generally allowed your firm to improve its tracking of supplier efficiency. Your firm had received national recognition in the purchasing and inventory control trade press for the improvements that the system bestowed on your firm's supply efforts. Despite the press recognition, the firm had released only information describing the total impact on the firm's operation and the benefits that had accrued since the proprietary system had been implemented. The firm had never released information that would have allowed the system to be duplicated easily by a competitor, or at least, you don't remember such a release. The discovery of the competitor's system came about when a supplier mentioned to one of your account managers that another of their customers, your major competitor, had brought on-line a computer system with functions similar to those of your system. The supplier was as impressed with the new system as he was with yours when it came on-line. The competitive advantage that your system had provided your firm apparently has been lost.

Things began to get real bad. Four days later, your director of the product development department called and reported to you that a new service your firm had planned to promote heavily has competition. It appears that your competitor has beaten you to market with a similar service. The competitive service's pricing structure and similarity to your as-yet-unannounced service are uncanny — especially because no other firm in your market area previously offered such a service. The coincidence that such a service accompanied with a pricing structure similar to your planned effort has been brought to market prior to your product introduction is almost beyond comprehension. It is as if the competitor had a pipeline into your strategic planning and is using your creativity and market know-how against you. How could such a coincidence occur? Thinking back to your management education, you cannot recall any discussions concerning market coincidences or how they might arise. More importantly, you don't recall any case studies that detailed how to best deal with such coincidences. You really began to feel ill.

The month ended on a horrible note. Yesterday, besides bringing an end to the calendar month, the work day brought to light a new revelation that could not be explained away by a possibility of coincidence. The director of your marketing research department was waiting in your office when you arrived at work. Surely, a bad omen. The director reported that a pseudonym attached to a post office box belonging to your firm received a promotional mailing from a competitor. The pseudonym intentionally had been listed among the firm's top customer prospect list several years ago. The pseudonym and box address were created by the research department and were used to verify and track delivery of promotional and account mailings, questionnaires, and for miscellaneous research purposes. Besides being a pseudonym, the name is basically a secret that is not known outside of the department, let alone outside of the business. Because it had never been revealed to anyone beyond a few of the firm's employees, its appearance in a promotional mailing by your competitor is surprising, if not outright bewildering. The director of research is perplexed as to how the competitor acquired the pseudonym and box number. The director can offer no explanation as to how the name and box number came to be on another firm's mailing list.

It finally dawns on you. Somehow, your competitor has come into possession of some of your firm's business secrets. In fact, your competitor seems to be in possession of your firm's most valuable, proprietary information. Marketing research results, information and decisions related to location research, computer system design, customer names and related information, detailed marketing and advertising campaign plans, and who knows what other types of valuable, proprietary information obviously have been leaked to your competitor. You wonder who could be responsible for such damaging leaks. Could a current employee be giving the information away? Could an employee be selling it? Could a disgruntled former employee be engaged in efforts aimed at trying to exact revenge on your firm by giving away its valuable secrets that serve as the basis for its competitive advantage in the market? Could a former employee be using your valuable, secret information as a means for advancement while working for his or her new employer? To be in possession of such information and to be able to make use of it to the advantage of another firm potentially would place a new employee in an enviable and indispensable position. Perhaps that's the answer to the puzzle. Maybe a former employee is responsible for all of this. A former employee may be giving the information away or using the information, and that individual is responsible for your firm's problems. Then, a horrible thought hits you. The thought creeps over you and makes you all the more uncomfortable. Maybe, as a member of your firm's top management, you could be responsible. Did you make an effort to insure that such information was secure and that reasonable measures were taken to protect the information? Were steps taken that reasonably could be expected to preclude the information falling into the possession of others? You may be responsible because you failed to take reasonable efforts to protect such information and prevent it from falling into the hands of your competitors.

TRADE SECRETS BACKGROUND

The activities of business professionals cause them to be exposed regularly to information that might be construed to be trade secrets. Such secrets can take on many forms, including, but not limited to, confidential customer lists, business research results, proprietary process information, formulas, and privileged market data. A plan that provides for adequate protection of business secrets should be a product of every firm's strategic planning initiatives. To assure that a firm is in a position to obtain the maximum level of legal support available for the protection of its secrets (and it is important to realize that such secrets can be legally protected), its planning should take into account the provisions of the Uniform Trade Secrets Act (UTSA) and lessons learned from relevant legal cases involving trade secrets.

In recent years, numerous suits seeking injunctions barring the use of and damages for the misappropriation or theft of trade secrets have been prosecuted. Although many of the firms involved in these suits could be classified as high technology firms (for example, IBM, NCR, General Electric), many are not. The industries in which organizations have sought redress under trade secrets laws represent a variety of business and professional pursuits, including firms in the health and medical care field, personnel placement firms, insurance companies, composite materials construction, transportation firms, restaurants, entertainment providers, and even firms involved in the cosmetics business. The threat of trade secrets misappropriation is significant, and instances of misappropriation appear to be on the rise.

Firms that rely on their trade secrets to give them competitive advantages need to have a systematic plan of action that will provide for the adequate protection of their secrets. Not surprisingly, almost every business executive ensures that steps are taken to protect cash and other physical assets. Often to their dismay, executives of many firms have discovered, too late, that it is just as important to provide for the protection of intangible assets such as valuable trade secrets as it is to provide for the protection of physical assets. Indeed, protection that insures the continued secrecy and proprietary nature of intangible assets is often necessary for the well-being and long-run competitive stature of a firm.

Firms that possess valuable information that is viewed as crucial to their continued success need to have a systematic plan of action that identifies, protects, and monitors the continued protection of that information. The plan of action outlined herein should assist executives in their planning to provide for the maximum level of legal protection available for trade secrets, especially as it relates to conducting business in jurisdictions that have adopted the UTSA.

WHAT ABOUT TRADEMARKS,
PATENTS, AND COPYRIGHTS?

Firms in the United States have enjoyed different types of legal protection for their intellectual properties for years. Trademarks, copyrights, and patents are among the legal instruments that have allowed varying levels, types, and lengths of federally protected property rights. These forms of federal protection, however, have weaknesses, which result in their providing an inadequate level of protection for proprietary business and competitive information.

For instance, patent laws in the United States provide inventors or, more specifically, an invention's registered patent owner protection from infringement for a maximum of 20 years. To gain the maximum legal protection offered under U.S. patent laws, it is necessary to publicly disclose the "secrets" inherent in the product or process for which a patent is sought. A patent application contains and makes available information that may have been construed to be secret by the applicant but obviously is no longer secret, because any secrets are detailed in the application. In cases in which the courts decide that the Patent Office improperly issued a patent, the invention would have been disclosed to competitors, to the detriment of the patent owner. Further, U.S. patent law offers no protection for secrets such as customer lists, market research results, or other information items not typically construed as involving physical products or processes. Indeed, it is this type of information that most concerns business professionals as they seek protection for their proprietary trade secrets.

It should be noted that patent protection and trade secret protection, although both concern ownership rights and property use exclusivity, are, themselves, mutually exclusive (patent application requires the public disclosure of information, which would invalidate claims of trade secret protection, and the handling of information as trade secrets makes it virtually impossible to create a valid patent claim). The owner of valuable, secret information is free to choose trade secret protection over patent protection if it is appropriate and the information owner so desires. In the landmark decision found in *Kewanee Oil Co. v. Bicron Corp.* (1973), it was held that neither the patent clause in the U.S. Constitution nor federal patent statutes preempt trade secrets protection provided through state laws. This holds true for both patentable and nonpatentable information. As is often the case for trade secrets, patent laws are inapplicable to trade secrets protection and, therefore, business executives need to look to state trade secrets laws to provide the level of protection desired.

Copyright laws do provide for the legal protection of copyrightable materials. The length of time that copyright laws extend protection and exclusivity to registered copyright owners far surpasses the length of time registered patent owners can enjoy their property rights as granted through patent law. For instance, an author registering a copyright on a written work today will enjoy the protection of federal copyright laws for the rest of the author's life plus a period extending 50 years beyond the author's life. In other words, the heirs to the owner of a registered copyright will continue to own the copyright to the materials for 50 years after the death of the individual who registered the work. This long ownership period stands in stark contrast to the relatively short 20 years granted by patent laws.

A weakness of copyright laws similar to the inherent weakness of patent laws concerns the public disclosure of the information to be registered. To register a copyright with the Library of Congress, copies of the material to be copyrighted must be submitted with the copyright application. It is not likely that a business executive would want to copyright a customer list, because the names would become a matter of public record. It would become increasingly laborious, time-consuming, and potentially expensive if, every time a new customer name was added to a specific list, a new copyright application were to be filed. In any case, registering a copyright moves secret information to the public domain. Firms obtaining the list could make sales calls on the customers. It is no longer secret.

Another, less obvious weakness is that copyright laws protect the specific, tangible incarnation of a work, not an idea behind the work. If copyright laws extended their protection to ideas, then there would be few works of literature in modern life. For instance, if ideas were copyrightable, there would likely exist few, perhaps only one, story in which the "butler" was the protaganist. There could be only one movie about a brave soldier in a particular war, about a police detective, about lovers from families who despise one another, one television talk show, one country love song involving a cowgirl and a pickup truck, one song that could be described as the blues, or, worse, only one soap opera on television. Thus, copyright laws do not provide protection for valuable information that is secret and which most business owners and executives desire to have remain secret.

What about the remaining bastion of federal proprietary property rights, trademark laws? Do trademark laws encompass trade secrets protection? In short, no. The Lanham Act is the federal law that established and guides trademarking efforts in the United States. Under federal trademark law, a business or individual registering a trademark with the U.S. Patent Office obtains a license of exclusivity for the material that is granted a trademark. In most instances, a trademark license belongs to the registering party forever. Exceptions to this perpetual license exist. For example, a trademark owner may lose a trademark if a federal judge declares the trademark to have been so entwined in our lexicon as to have become a generic word. Aspirin and nylon are examples of such a judicial declaration. They are words that at one time were trademarked but later were declared to be generic and put into the public domain.

As one may surmise by these two examples, trademark law is aimed at protecting the exclusivity of brand names, symbols, or other identifying information of a business or product, not trade secrets. Customer lists, account information, process secrets, marketing research results, and a host of other types of information that may be construed to be trade secrets cannot be trademarked and, therefore, are ineligible for protection under the Lanham Act.

Thus, if patent, copyright, and trademark laws do not provide businesses with protection for their trade secrets, how does one go about protecting such proprietary information? Given that federal laws do not adequately provide for the protection of trade secrets, one must look to the laws of the individual states for guidance and any legal protection provided by state laws.

Business executives utilize many tools of the trade that have value and provide them competitive advantages. Tools such as confidential and detailed customer account data, business or management controls, market knowledge, and other "unpatentable" assets often are as valuable as any physical product, process, or technique that may qualify for patent registration and its accompanying legal protection and promise of market exclusivity. Acknowledging the existence of such trade secrets and recognizing the need to provide adequate and consistent protection for these secrets, the National Conference of Commissioners on Uniform State Laws approved and recommended for adoption the UTSA in 1979. The UTSA later was amended by the commissioners in 1985.

The commissioners are charged with developing uniform laws that will provide for consistent legal treatment in every state relative to those needs that transcend state boundaries but for which inadequate protection exists at the federal level. The Uniform Commercial Code and the Uniform Child Custody Jurisdiction Act are examples of the commissioners' efforts. The UTSA was developed and proposed for the purpose of providing consistent treatment and protection of trade secrets. Because federal statutes do not preempt protection afforded trade secrets through state laws, it is important that executives understand the UTSA. Providing for the protection of trade secrets through a comprehensive plan of action that adheres to expectations as embodied in the UTSA and that takes into account the findings of relevant court cases should be viewed as an increasingly important component in one's competitive strategy.

Such a strategy would involve a seven-step plan of action aimed at providing for and maintaining the secrecy surrounding one's trade secrets. Each of the seven steps requires forethought, an understanding of the UTSA, and a recognition that, if one truly desires to protect one's trade secrets, a proactive strategy must be undertaken. Merely sitting back and hoping for the best will not protect one's trade secrets and surely will not garner legal protection or remedy should such an effort be deemed necessary. The steps in a strategic plan aimed at protecting trade secrets must receive sufficient thought and effort so as to provide the basis for any legal protection sought under the UTSA or similar state statutes in those states that have not yet adopted the act. Because the cost of trade secrets misappropriation is billions of dollars annually, the importance of providing adequate security for trade secrets and insuring that any protection efforts are construed as meeting the expectations of the UTSA cannot be emphasized too much.

The first step in the plan[1] involves the need for the creation and maintenance of a climate or atmosphere of confidentiality surrounding the firm's secrets. A climate of confidentiality will help insure that employees recognize that valuable information is being compiled or handled and that management expects employees to treat the information at hand as a valuable secret. Employees working in a climate of confidentiality arguably are more attuned to the need for maintaining secrecy of sensitive information on which the firm depends for its success. Such a climate hopefully would foster efforts for secrets protection that goes beyond those prescribed by management policy. It would serve to inform and remind employees about the critical role they play in the continued success of the firm. As will be seen, the creation and maintenance of an atmosphere of confidentiality can result from a variety of efforts and will play an important role in the strategic protection efforts of a firm's secrets.

After or almost simultaneously with developing a climate of confidentiality in a firm's environment, the firm's management will need to delineate which information it possesses that it considers to be a trade secret. If reasonable protective measures are to be taken, they will need to be aimed at protecting specific information in the possession of the firm. Such a delineation will insure that sufficient steps are taken to protect the specific information and serve to alert employees about which information the firm considers to be a valuable secret. The firm's management needs to be specific in its policy statements and in its strategic efforts to define the scope of its secrets. A noncompete agreement embodying company policy that restricts employees from using any information acquired in an employee's current employment in a future employment situation would not be deemed reasonable, because most of what one learns at work would not be secret, and, therefore, would be unenforceable. This points out the importance of specifying which information the firm possesses that it considers to be its secrets and, once information is so identified, taking proactive steps to protect the secrets.

The third step in a strategic effort aimed at protecting trade secrets will involve a determination as to the value of the information considered to be a trade secret. The UTSA and many other state trade secrets acts offer protection for trade secrets that are deemed to have independent economic value. If a firm's secrets do not possess value, the courts will not extend their protection to the secrets. By delineating the specific information the firm considers to be a trade secret, the firm then can assess the value of the information. The information must have value, significant value, if it is to garner legal protection. Value can take many forms, but the courts expect to see independent economic value at the heart of any information considered a trade secret and for which legal protection is sought. By assessing the value of any trade secrets a firm claims to possess, the management also can assess the reasonableness of any efforts implemented to protect the secrets.

The fourth step involves a determination that, one may argue, needs to be made early in the firm's efforts, that is, the information must be assessed as to its secrecy. Trade secrets by definition are secrets. It may sound trite, but the information must be secret to be a protectable trade secret. At first consideration, such a concern seems almost trivial, but secrecy lies at the heart of trade secrets law. If information is not secret, then it cannot garner protection as a trade secret, regardless of its value. After delineating which information it considers secret and assuring that the information is valuable, a firm needs to assess realistically the secrecy of the information. Implementing expensive procedures to protect nonsecret information and safeguard it as if it were a secret could be a waste of funds and effort. Most information that firms possess and utilize on a daily basis does not qualify as legally protectable trade secrets. For instance, double entry bookkeeping and basic chemical formulas used by a particular firm would not qualify as trade secrets, because double entry accounting procedures and basic chemical formulas are well-known. The UTSA offers protection for secrets, not for commonly known information.

Assuming the firm finds that the information is valuable and secret and has cultivated a climate of confidentiality surrounding the information, a reasonable plan for safeguarding the information must be developed. The plan should insure the maintenance of secrecy surrounding the information. The plan should be reevaluated periodically with respect to its effectiveness in making sure it continues to provide the level of security deemed appropriate given the value of the information the plan intends to protect and the circumstances in which the firm operates. The plan should provide for a variety of factors to maintain security, not the least of which will involve the designation of who among a firm's employees will have access to the secrets and under what circumstances access will be allowed. The UTSA specifies that trade secrets must be subject to reasonable efforts, given the circumstances, to maintain their secrecy. Executives necessarily have to provide reasonable protection for their secrets.

The sixth step in the process emphasizes the role that good legal counsel can play in the preparation of a firm's strategic planning involving the protection of trade secrets. As in any circumstance involving the law, one needs to seek out and obtain competent legal counsel. The facts that the UTSA is not yet universally adopted, that some minor differences exist among some of the states adopting the act, and that laws change over time all point to the necessity of seeking legal counsel when preparing a plan to protect trade secrets. This step involves assessing one's protection plan in light of the specifics of the UTSA and subsequent court cases filed pursuant to its auspices.

Finally, the last step in preparing a plan of action relative to protecting a firm's trade secrets involves the implementation and enforcement of the plan. Numerous firms in various industries lost available legal protection that the UTSA may have been able to offer had their executives implemented and sustained an adequate climate of confidentiality. A plan not implemented has the same effect as having no plan and may cause a firm desiring legal protection or seeking legal remedy for a misappropriation to fail in its efforts.

NOTE

1. The plan presented here was discussed in Michael C. Budden, Robert C. Lake, and John W. Yeargain. 1995. "Strategic Planning for Protection of Business Secrets Under the Uniform Trade Secrets Act." *Journal of Managerial Issues*, 7(3): 343–57.

2

The Uniform Trade Secrets Act

As of this date, 40 states and the District of Columbia have adopted the Uniform Trade Secrets Act (UTSA) (Table 2.1). Minor variations exist between the various states' versions, but the variations primarily center on the names of the acts (for example, Louisiana's version is named the Louisiana Trade Secrets Act) and, as one would expect, the effective dates of implementation. Additionally, as will be noted in a later chapter, California's act embodies a small but potentially significant change in the definition of a trade secret. Overall, the differences are minimal across the jurisdictions that have adopted the UTSA, and consistency in the treatment of trade secrets in the courts has significantly improved.

It is probable that additional states will adopt the UTSA in the near future. Until then, executives operating in states that have not yet adopted the UTSA will find the plan of action and court decisions detailed here of potential use in their planning efforts. Still, business executives will need to be aware of their specific states' trade secrets acts and relevant court decisions and plan accordingly. Once the UTSA becomes law nationwide, the ability of executives to provide adequate protection of trade secrets in the United States will be simplified.

Because the law is a relatively recent phenomenon, most of the relevant cases have made their way through the courts in the past ten years. These cases are helping to shape the understanding and scope of the act and, along with the UTSA itself and relevant commissioners' notes, are the

TABLE 2.1
Jurisdictions that Have Adopted the Uniform Trade Secrets Act

Alabama	Minnesota
Alaska	Mississippi
Arizona	Missouri
Arkansas	Montana
California	Nebraska
Colorado	Nevada
Connecticut	New Hampshire
Delaware	New Mexico
District of Columbia	North Dakota
Florida	Ohio
Georgia	Oklahoma
Hawaii	Oregon
Idaho	Rhode Island
Illinois	South Carolina
Indiana	South Dakota
Iowa	Utah
Kansas	Virginia
Kentucky	Washington
Louisiana	West Virginia
Maine	Wisconsin
Maryland	

Source: *Uniform Laws Annotated*, Vol. 14, *Civil, Procedural, and Remedial Laws*, 1996 Cumulative Annual Packet Part. St. Paul, MN: West.

basis for the strategic plan presented here. This plan will assist business executives in their efforts to protect their firms' property rights in valuable, secret information construed to be trade secrets under the UTSA.

Even in those jurisdictions that have not yet adopted the UTSA, the steps proposed here will provide guidance in establishing policies and procedures helpful in safeguarding a firm's intellectual property. Business owners and executives are especially vulnerable to the problems inherent in trade secrets ownership, because many of the activities and proprietary information of businesses can be protected only as trade secrets (for example, customer lists and account histories, marketing research results, product specifications), not as patentable or copyrightable information.

Once the UTSA becomes adopted universally by the 49 states whose laws are based on the English common law, consistent treatment in the courts relative to trade secrets protection will be essentially assured. It is significant to note that Louisiana is among the states that already have adopted the act, because its laws historically are derived from the Napoleonic Code (civil code) and do not necessarily conform to the English common law, from which the other states' laws have evolved. The UTSA holds the promise of providing consistent protection of trade secrets for firms operating in all 50 states. Because federal statutes currently do not preempt protection afforded trade secrets through state laws, the importance of understanding the UTSA and other relevant state acts is of paramount importance if strategic efforts by management to protect proprietary properties are to be effective.

The UTSA basically encompasses 12 sections. Each section has its own purpose or provision. Among the items provided for in these sections are those that define trade secrets and other terms utilized in the act; allow for injunctive relief; provide for damages, including the potential for assessments of punitive damages and potential recovery of attorney fees; provide for court efforts to maintain secrecy surrounding the trade secret; provide for a statute of limitations that limits the time during which actions can be brought before a court; and provide for a variety of other stipulations relative to the act and its enforcement. The text of the UTSA, shown in italics, follows, with explanatory comments or cases provided for each section.

THE UNIFORM TRADE SECRETS ACT

Section 1. Definitions

As used in this Act, unless the context requires otherwise:

(1) *"Improper means" includes theft, bribery, misrepresentation, breach or inducement of a breach of duty to maintain secrecy, or espionage through electronic or other means;*

(2) *"Misappropriation" means:*

  (i) *acquisition of a trade secret of another by a person who knows or has reason to know that the trade secret was acquired by improper means; or*

  (ii) *disclosure or use of a trade secret of another without express or implied consent by a person who*

   (A) *used improper means to acquire knowledge of the trade secret; or*

   (B) *at the time of disclosure or use, knew or had reason to know that his knowledge of the trade secret was*

> (I)   *derived from or through a person who had utilized improper means to acquire it;*
>
> (II)   *acquired under circumstances giving rise to a duty to maintain its secrecy or limit its use; or*
>
> (III) *derived from or through a person who owed a duty to the person seeking relief to maintain its secrecy or limit its use; or*
>
> (C) *before a material change of his position, knew or had reason to know that it was a trade secret and that knowledge of it had been acquired by accident or mistake.*

(3) "Person" means a natural person, corporation, business trust, estate, trust, partnership, association, joint venture, government, governmental subdivision or agency, or any other legal or commercial entity.

(4) "Trade secret" means information, including a formula, pattern, compilation, program, device, method, technique, or process, that:

> (i)   *derives independent economic value, actual or potential, from not being generally known to, and not being readily ascertainable by proper means by, other persons who can obtain economic value from its disclosure or use, and*
>
> (ii) *is the subject of efforts that are reasonable under the circumstances to maintain its secrecy.*

In Section 1, the definitions embodied within the act explain the major terms and the delineation of those terms within the meaning of the act. Although all of the definitions hold important meaning and play a significant role in explaining the scope of the act, the first definition that needs to be addressed here briefly is the definition of a trade secret. As will be seen in later chapters, the question of what constitutes a trade secret is often at the center of cases alleging misappropriation. A trade secret is information "that derives independent economic value, actual or potential, from not being generally known to, and not being readily ascertainable by proper means by, other persons who can obtain economic value from its disclosure or use, and is the subject of efforts that are reasonable under the circumstances to maintain its secrecy."

As can be seen here, three major factors determine the existence of a trade secret. First, the information must have independent economic value, actual or potential. Information that lacks value cannot qualify as a trade secret. As will be seen in a later chapter, the concept of having value implies that the information has significant value. Second, the information must not be generally known to others and not be readily established by proper means. If information is generally known, it cannot be a secret; thus, it cannot be a trade secret. Further, the definition says that the information cannot be "readily ascertainable by proper means." This implies that, if one could easily determine the secret through legal means even though at the time it was not generally known, it would not be construed as a trade secret under the UTSA. Further, the concept of "proper means" implies a legal establishment of the information. An armed robbery that results in the stealing of one's trade secrets is an extreme example of what is not meant by being "readily ascertainable by proper means." Finally, the third factor that would need to exist in order to construe information to be a protectable trade secret is whether or not the information was subject to reasonable efforts, under the circumstances, to maintain secrecy. The act expects that, if one has valuable, secret information that gives one a competitive advantage, efforts will be made to protect the information and to maintain its secrecy. In many of the cases that have made it through the courts relative to trade secrets misappropriation, the question as to whether a trade secret has been misappropriated has hinged on whether or not a trade secret exists in the first place. If a trade secret is not shown to exist, then it stands to reason that a misappropriation cannot have occurred.

In *Corrosion Specialties and Supply, Inc., v. Dicharry et al.* the question of the existence of a trade secret was central to the charges brought concerning misappropriation. Corrosion Specialties is engaged in the distribution of large industrial valves. For several years, it had been the sole U.S. distributor of a valve produced by a German manufacturing firm. The class of valves in question had been on the market for over 50 years and, therefore, was not protected by patents. In an attempt to remain price-competitive, Corrosion Specialties tried, unsuccessfully, to enter a joint production agreement with the German manufacturer that would have resulted in the valves being produced locally and, as a result, potentially priced more competitively. When the German manufacturer declined to enter the joint venture, Corrosion Specialties sought out a domestic manufacturer to produce the valves.

As a result, Corrosion Specialties proposed to the defendants that they produce the valves for it to distribute. Reportedly, at the time, the defendants were not knowledgeable about the type of valve Corrosion desired. Examples of the valves and associated design drawings were delivered to the defendants by representatives of Corrosion. In addition, information on modifications to the original valves that were desired by Corrosion were delivered to the defendants. Corrosion mentioned that the modifications were needed to conform to recent government regulations relative to the design and manufacture of valves involved in the transport of certain industrial products. The defendants began plans to finalize the design and prepared to manufacture the valves. Meanwhile, Corrosion Specialties' principal and the defendants had been engaged in oral discussions concerning the agreement. The discussions were terminated when the two sides could not agree on the specific terms of the production contract.

It was reported that the defendants continued their efforts to design and manufacture the valves without the cooperation of Corrosion Specialties. A few months later, a suit was filed by the plaintiff, seeking injunctive relief and claiming that the defendants had, among other charges, misappropriated its trade secrets. The trial court found for the plaintiff and issued an injunction prohibiting the defendants from pursuing efforts to design and manufacture the valves in question. Among the trial court's finding was that the valves, design drawings, and their design changes were protectable trade secrets under the law.

On appeal, the finding that a trade secret existed was found to be in error. The Fifth Circuit Court of Appeal in Louisiana disagreed that the valves and the planned changes to the valves were protectable trade secrets. It noted that the valves had been on the market for decades. Therefore, they were readily obtainable, and any secrets they might have possessed were readily ascertainable. In addition, the changes that were desired in order to comply with new government regulations concerning safety and applicability were public knowledge, because the new regulations could be obtained, and were readily obtainable, from the agencies involved. In short, the valves were not a trade secret. The changes required by government agencies to comply with new regulations were not a trade secret. The court of appeal found that the information in question was not a trade secret under the Louisiana UTSA.

The term "improper means," as one might expect, includes the concept of theft, bribery, and espionage. However, it also includes, as is seen in many of the cases, a breach of duty to maintain secrecy, which may arise from the specific action of an individual who breaks a written or oral contract or an implied duty to maintain secrets entrusted to that individual.

Further, the idea that a misappropriation occurs through the disclosure or use of a trade secret without the express or implied consent of the owner will surprise few. Included in the definition of misappropriation under the act is the acquisition of a trade secret by a person who knows or has reason to know that the trade secret was acquired by improper means.

The Supreme Court of Alabama addressed such issues in the case of *Imed Corporation et al. v. Systems Engineering Associates et al.* In *Imed,* the state high court specifically addressed two questions that help to shed light on the act's expectation that individuals who know or should have reason to know that they are using trade secrets misappropriated by a third person can be considered liable for the unapproved use of the information.

The two questions centered around when and if a third party is liable for using or disclosing a trade secret that had been misappropriated by another. Specifically, the court was asked to determine if an individual is liable with respect to the following two scenarios.

1. Can a defendant be held liable for the continued use or disclosure of a trade secret after receiving notice of an alleged misappropriation by a third party when the information had been obtained before the defendant knew or should have known that the information was a trade secret that had been misappropriated?

2. Can a defendant be held liable for the use or disclosure of a trade secret if he or she received the information without notice of it having been misappropriated but used or disclosed the secret for the first time after receiving notice that the information in question was a protectable trade secret?

The court agreed with Systems Engineering Associates' assertion that a person can be held liable under Alabama law (the UTSA) if he or she knew or should have known at the time the information was learned that it had been misappropriated by a third person. The court noted that Alabama's statute specifies that a person who discloses or uses the trade secret of another, without a privilege to do so, is liable to the other for misappropriation of the trade secret if that person learned the trade secret from a third person and knew or should have known that the information was a trade secret and that the trade secret had been misappropriated. The unambiguous wording in Alabama's UTSA did not give the court room to ascertain a judicial interpretation as to what might be meant by the provisions embodied in the statute. The statute is clearly stated and, therefore, is clear to interpret.

As one might surmise, when a statute is constructed clearly, as was the case here, the words used in the statute must be given their plain and commonly understood meaning in a court proceeding. When such is the case, a court must interpret the language of an act exactly as given, keeping the intent of the legislature fully intact. The court indicated that to read the wording of the act and to try and ascertain another interpretation, given the clarity of the statute's wording, would be difficult and counter to a court's charge. The court's conclusion was to support the fundamental trade secrets doctrine that individual property rights in trade secrets should be protected from misappropriation. The court noted that the wording of the act is not ambiguous in stating that an individual who uses or discloses a trade secret is liable for the misappropriation if the individual knew or should have known that the information acquired from a third party was a trade secret that had been misappropriated from its rightful owner. The answer to both questions raised in the case is a definite yes. Finally, based on the wording of the court's decision, it should be noted that the source of a notice of a misappropriation is not germane to the discussion of whether or not someone is liable. If one receives sufficient notice of a relevant misappropriation by another and continues to use or disclose the secret, then liability for the use or disclosure can arise.

The definition of a trade secret within the act encompasses information that includes "a formula, pattern, compilation, program, device, method, technique, or process" that possesses independent economic value and is the subject of efforts that are reasonable under the circumstances to maintain its secrecy. In the case *205 Corporation v. Brandow et al.* a question arose as to whether food recipes used in commerce could qualify as trade secrets under Iowa's UTSA.

The Tavern Restaurant, a subsidiary of the 205 Corporation, needed a manager. Brandow was hired to manage the restaurant, which was known for its pizza and a line of specialty sandwiches referred to as grinder sandwiches. The 205 Corporation provided the pizza sauce, crust mix, and grinder sandwiches to the tavern. It was reported that the recipes for the secret sauce and grinder sandwiches were proprietary, because they were known only to the current president of the corporation and the former owner of the restaurant. The pizza crust recipe was known to several individuals, some of whom no longer worked for the tavern. The 205 Corporation purchased the recipes as part of the goodwill associated with the restaurant at the time it purchased the restaurant.

Sometime later, Brandow was terminated as the manager by the 205 Corporation. He went to work for another restaurant, where it was alleged he provided the pizza and grinder sandwich recipes to his new employer. Shortly thereafter, suit was filed containing the claims that the recipes were trade secrets that had been misappropriated. To be considered a trade secret, the recipes would have to be information that is not generally known or readily ascertainable, possesses independent economic value, and is the subject of efforts that are reasonable under the circumstances to maintain their secrecy.

Testimony by the former owner of the restaurant indicated he felt that the recipes were among the more valuable assets of the business when he sold it. Normally, the recipes were secured in a safe deposit box when not in use. The manager was given instructions as to the need to provide adequate security for the recipes and cautioned that the recipes were not to be left unsecured or otherwise accessible to others. In contrast to the procedures surrounding the security of the sauce, procedures for securing the crust recipe were less stringent. Because the crust needed to be made on a daily basis and because of the labor-intensive nature of the crust-making procedure, all tavern employees became aware of the crust recipe and procedure.

A key to understanding the Supreme Court's decision was the term "reasonable under the circumstances." The hectic, close environment of a kitchen requires that much interaction take place to assure success. Given the needs associated with the crust preparation process, the high court found that the restaurant's secrecy procedures were reasonable under the circumstances. In addition, testimony was presented that the ingredients in the recipes could be determined only through an expensive analytic procedure not commonly available, but even then, the actual process involved in combining the ingredients that resulted in the uniqueness of the recipes would not be discoverable through proper means.

In short, the recipes were found to be secret information not known to or readily ascertainable by others, to hold independent economic value, and to be the subject of efforts that were reasonable under the circumstances to preserve their secrecy. The affirmation by the Supreme Court that the recipes were trade secrets should not surprise many.

An individual who acquires a trade secret by accident or mistake and knew or had reason to know that the information was a trade secret and knowingly uses the secret to the detriment of the owner may be guilty of misappropriation, especially if the acquiring individual had a duty to maintain confidentiality. As a result, an employee who knowingly divulges trade secret information belonging to an employer to whom a duty of secrecy is owed, even though the information was acquired by accident during the course of that individual's employment, can be guilty of misappropriating the firm's trade secrets.

What constitutes a "person" under the auspices of the UTSA is clearly spelled out in this section of the act. It includes people as well as a variety of governmental or business relationships and entities. Corporations, partnerships, and other forms of business enterprise are included in the definition and, therefore, enjoy both the benefits and the responsibilities inherent within the scope of the UTSA. In at least one court case in which the definition of a "person" was questioned, the court seemed to take a broad perspective of a "person" in light of the act's rather broad treatment in its definition.

Section 2. Injunctive Relief

(a) Actual or threatened misappropriation may be enjoined. Upon application to the court, an injunction shall be terminated when the trade secret has ceased to exist, but the injunction may be continued for an additional reasonable period of time in order to eliminate commercial advantage that otherwise would be derived from the misappropriation.

(b) If the court determines that it would be unreasonable to prohibit future use, an injunction may condition future use upon payment of a reasonable royalty for no longer than the period of time the use could have been prohibited.

(c) In appropriate circumstances, affirmative acts to protect a trade secret may be compelled by court order.

Recognition of the fact that unjust enrichment should be precluded in cases in which misappropriations occur, the courts are given wide latitude relative to enjoining those who may make use of misappropriated secrets. The act states that actual misappropriation may be enjoined. The potential for injunctions to bar the misuse of one's trade secrets is vital to the protection afforded the owners of such proprietary property.

One should note, though, that the word "may" in this section of the act is not an imperative order for injunctions to ensue merely because one believes that a misappropriation is occurring. Courts are given latitude in deciding whether or not to enjoin one's actions and will take into account, among other factors, the potential for irreparable harm; the potential impact on the parties involved, given the facts before the court; and other matters to be mentioned later. Preliminary injunctions are of special concern to many in business, because they are requested prior to an actual trial on all of the merits of the case. In the case of *Capital Tool and Manufacturing Company, Inc. v. Maschinenfabrik Herkules et al.*, the delineation between the words "may" and "must" became central to the discussion as to why a preliminary injunction might not ensue in cases alleging trade secrets misappropriation. It needs to be noted that a preliminary injunction's purpose essentially is to maintain the status quo or relative positions of the parties involved until a trial on the merits of the case can be heard.

In *Capital Tool*, a former employee who was involved in the development of control systems for the firm left and went to work for a customer of the firm, Herkules, after relations between the two firms apparently soured. The former employee was an engineer who reportedly devoted most of his employment at Capital Tool to the development of control systems for equipment purchased by Herkules. After the relations between the two firms apparently soured, Herkules reported that it considered a contract between the two firms as being terminated. The contract had stipulated, among other things, that Capital Tool would provide Herkules with mill equipment and allied control systems for a period of up to ten years. Shortly after the announcement of the contract termination, the employee left and accepted a position as president and coowner of a newly formed division of Herkules. As president of Herkules Controls, the engineer and the division were charged with developing a control system for a piece of machinery purchased while the contract between the firms was still in force.

Capital Tool quickly filed suit seeking a preliminary injunction barring the former employee from working for the new division of Herkules and barring the use, by both the former employee and the new Herkules division, of information alleged to be trade secrets. The suit claimed that there were violations of contractual obligations and violations of its rights under Virginia's UTSA.

Noting that Herkules's new division and its president were developing controls for machinery already sold by Capital Tool, were not competing with Capital Tool or threatening to compete with Capital Tool, and were not in a position to inflict competitive injuries on Capital Tool and that no irreparable injury would be inflicted on Capital Tool pending a trial on its merits, the lower court denied the request for a preliminary injunction. The United States Court of Appeals for the Fourth Circuit affirmed the lower court's decision, noting that the court was acting within its bounds of discretion, because the UTSA allows the granting of injunctions, not orders them. Specifically, the court of appeals delineated between the words "may" and "must" and affirmed the court's decision not to issue an injunction.

It is especially interesting to note that Section 2 of the UTSA not only allows for injunctions against actual and ongoing misappropriations of trade secrets but also allows for the granting of an injunction where a "threatened misappropriation" is likely to occur. This is good news for businesses finding themselves potentially at risk of losing valuable secrets through the actions of former employees to whom secrets were entrusted. Indeed, an article in *The Wall Street Journal* reported that IBM filed suit against one of its former vice presidents in order to enjoin him from using trade secrets belonging to the computer giant. The report stated that the former executive had not been accused of any wrongdoing or stealing of secrets but that the case was being pursued because executives at IBM perceived his departure as a potentially serious threat to its trade secrets. The suit and warnings to several other former IBM employees to maintain confidentiality of the firm's secrets, which were issued almost concurrently, were perceived as unprecedented actions by some, and in some ways, perhaps, the moves were unprecedented. However, the UTSA allows threatened misappropriations to be enjoined, so it should not surprise many that firms are pursuing such efforts aimed at preventing secrets misuse.

In a relevant case that has already made it through the Indiana legal system, *Ackerman v. Kimball International, Inc.*, Kimball sought to enjoin a former employee from using or otherwise misappropriating information it claimed to be a trade secret. In this case, which will be detailed in a later chapter, the former employee was not accused of actually misappropriating or using the firm's trade secrets, but by virtue of his accepting employment at a competing firm in an alleged violation of a noncompete covenant, the former employee was perceived as posing a threat to the trade secrets of Kimball. Thus, the firm sought to enjoin his use of its secrets, a use that was perceived as a serious threat to the firm. The UTSA specifically states that a "threatened misappropriation may be enjoined." In this case, the former employer prevailed, because the court noted that the state's trade secrets law (the UTSA) allows that individuals seen as threatening misappropriation are subject to having such actions enjoined.

Section 3. Damages

(a) *In addition to or in lieu of injunctive relief, a complainant may recover damages for the actual loss caused by misappropriation. A complainant also may recover for the unjust enrichment caused by misappropriation that is not taken into account in computing damages for actual loss.*

(b) *If willful and malicious misappropriation exists, the court may award exemplary damages in an amount not exceeding twice any award made under subsection (a).*

One of the specific areas under the UTSA is its prescribed handling of damages in cases in which misappropriation is found to occur. It is also one of the areas about which business executives need to be especially concerned, because the act itself is concerned specifically with the misappropriation of "valuable" information. As can be seen in Section 3, a complainant may recover damages for the actual loss of the misappropriation as well as for any unjust enrichment found to occur that was not taken into account in computing damages for actual loss. As can be expected, this puts the onus on the complainant to have calculated the value of the loss and, in so doing, the value of unjust enrichment (if any) acquired by those misappropriating any secrets that are in question. The value of the information must be significant, and firms arguing misappropriation need to be in a position of proving such value.

The courts also are given flexibility in awarding exemplary damages in cases in which "willful and malicious" misappropriation is shown to exist. In such cases, the courts may award exemplary damages of up to twice any award given for actual loss or unjust enrichment.

In seeking damages for misappropriation of trade secrets, the information in question must have value. It is up to the complainant to specify and present evidence that indicates the amount of value inherent in the misappropriated information. Obviously, one would not be wise to file a complaint if misappropriated information was known to have no value. It will require an effort to calculate the value of the information and to pursue the protection of information possessing that value. Good cost accounting procedures may be relied upon in some instances when the actual cost (or value) of the information is in question.

Section 4. Attorney's Fees

If (i) a claim of misappropriation is made in bad faith, (ii) a motion to terminate an injunction is made or resisted in bad faith, or (iii) willful and malicious misappropriation exists, the court may award reasonable attorney's fees to the prevailing party.

Everyone involved in legal proceedings always wants to know about the awarding of attorney fees, because, in many instances, they can be quite substantial. Section 4 is relatively clear in stating that, in cases in which bad faith actions are pursued or willful and malicious misappropriation of trade secrets is found to exist, the court may award reasonable attorney's fees to the prevailing party. Such fees are in addition to any awards for actual loss and exemplary damages (if any) awarded under the act.

One case in which the court's finding of willful and malicious misappropriation serves as a textbook example of the awarding of damages was the case of *Central, Inc., v. Morrow et al.*, which occurred in South Dakota. Like many such cases, *Central* involved the actions of former employees that were seen as intruding on the trade secrets of their former employer. Central, Inc., is a member-based cooperative providing soil and crop testing and miscellaneous consultation services to farmers. In the course of their business affairs, the employees (consultants) are privy to a substantial variety of confidential and valuable information. This information to which the consultants were privy was considered to be a trade secret by Central. Employees were hired under an employment contract that contained noncompetition, nondisclosure covenants. The covenants provided that they would be effective for a period of one year following a termination or resignation of the employee and that, during that year, the employee was restrained from competing with Central in its "area of primary responsibility."

According to the record, the defendants began criticizing Central in the presence of their customers for several months prior to leaving its employ. They purportedly began to solicit business with the intent of moving that business away from Central and to the firms they were planning to start. It was reported that they used confidential information, records, customer lists, revenue reports, and a variety of other information belonging to Central in efforts seeking to obtain bank financing for their upstart ventures. Additionally, they were accused of using the confidential information in their own businesses after the three resigned from the firm and incorporated their own firms. The resignation of the three consultants left Central vulnerable, because the three represented over 40 percent of its consulting staff and their resignations came at a critical period when the firm's crop consulting contracts were in the process of being renewed for the following year. The defendants were successful in getting a majority of their former customers to allow their new firms to service their crop consulting needs.

Just a few weeks after their resignations and solicitation of Central's customers, Central filed suit, claiming that the defendants broke their noncompete and nondisclosure covenants and that they misappropriated the firm's trade secrets and claiming other charges relative to the actions of the three former employees. Central sought remedies, including an injunction of their competitive pursuits and punitive damages. In October of that year, the trial court preliminarily enjoined the three from continuing any competition with Central. Despite the order or, perhaps, in response to it, the three defendants transferred their stock in the competing businesses to their spouses or to the corporations. Their spouses became the sole shareholders in their respective corporations, became the sole officers, and became the directors. Through their spouses and under the auspices of their corporations, the defendants continued to service their customers, in apparent violation of the injunction. In subsequent court action, the court found the stock transfers and activities of the defendants to be attempts to evade the earlier injunction. They were found in contempt and reordered to obey the directives of the preliminary injunction. Perhaps unbelievably to some, the defendants reportedly continued to provide soil and crop consulting services in violation of both the preliminary injunction and the second, supplemental order.

At trial, Centrol had little trouble convincing the court that it had been victimized. The court awarded Centrol compensatory damages, punitive damages, attorney fees, and permanent injunctive relief. The total dollar award was in excess of $345,000 (of which $156,000 was for attorney fees). The defendants appealed, arguing that the court should have found the noncompete and nondisclosure covenants to be invalid, that compensatory and punitive damages were not appropriate, that they should not be jointly and severally liable for the award, that the damages were incorrectly calculated, and, perhaps, just as importantly, that no injunction should have ensued.

In reviewing the trial court's finding that the noncompete and nondisclose covenants were valid, the Supreme Court of South Dakota looked to the state's law relative to employment agreements. South Dakota law provides that employees may enter into noncompete covenants with employers so long as they do not restrict the employee's business or professional pursuits beyond a period of two years from a termination of the employment agreement. In addition, state law mandates that such covenants be specific as to their geographic coverage. Specifically, noncompete covenants should state the county, city, or other specified area to which they apply. Because the agreements specified that they were for a one year period, the time limit easily was within the two year maximum as state law allowed. The question of validity turned on the phrase "area of primary responsibility," which was intended to geographically define the market area to which the employee covenants applied. The Supreme Court found that the phrase was geographically definitive and noted that the trial court found that the defendants were aware of the market area under consideration because they personally had helped to prepare maps that delineated the area while they were employed at Centrol. Because the noncompete agreement met the requirements of time and geographic (place) specificity and because there was consideration in its establishment, the noncompete covenant was valid.

No arguments were advanced that contested the validity of the nondisclosure covenant. The Supreme Court considered the issue abandoned by the defendants, meaning that, if one is not willing to proffer an argument or stance as to why a decision is in error, the court will not do it for them. As a result, the trial court's finding that the nondisclosure agreement was valid was not found to have been in error.

Relative to the issue of damages, the Supreme Court found that the computation of compensatory damages had been incorrect. As a result, the total of punitive damages also needed to be recalculated. The amount of such damage calculation was remanded to the trial court. However, contrary to the defendants' arguments, the Supreme Court found that the awarding of punitive damages was not in error, given the totality of the charges and the actions of the individuals, including their competitive efforts following the issuance of the injunction. Additionally, the amount of the attorney fees awarded by the trial court was found not to be in error. The court concluded that the defendants conspired to enter into unfair competition with Centrol. Their actions as a group and individually resulted in damages to Centrol's operations. The court's conclusion that the defendants were jointly and severally liable for the entire award of compensatory damages and attorney fees was upheld. Finally, the issuance of the injunction also was upheld by the Supreme Court.

A case resulting in the calculation and imposition of a royalty as a remedy for the damages involving a misappropriation occurred in Virginia. *American Sales Corporation v. Adventure Travel, Inc.*, also saw the plaintiff firm seek punitive damages and attorney fees from a firm it felt had misappropriated its trade secrets. American Sales Corporation, a multilevel marketing company, sued a competitor who had contractually served its needs for a discount travel agency for breach of contract and misappropriation of trade secrets. In addition to compensatory damages, the plaintiff sought punitive damages and attorney fees it claimed were owed because of an action it perceived as a willful and malicious misappropriation of its secrets and a breach of contract.

As a multilevel marketer, American Sales promotes and sells a collection of discount services through distributors who, in turn, sell the firm's services and can recruit new distributors to sell the services the firm offers. As an aside, for those unfamiliar with multilevel marketing operations, multilevel marketing distributors typically receive not only a commission on their sales but also a lesser commission on the sales of their recruits. Thus, multilevel marketing is a very people-intensive, networking-involved endeavor that places great emphasis on recruiting and retaining distributors to insure an expanding customer base. In the current case, included as a part of the discount package sold through American distributors was a discount travel package previously contracted out to the defendant. The defendant provided the discount travel service to the customers of American until the expiration of its service agreement contract with American in early 1993. The contract included a provision that Adventure would maintain the confidentiality of the names of customers and it prohibited Adventure from using the list for its own business purposes. After the contract expired, it was reported that the defendant initiated its own multilevel marketing network and began offering services very similar to American's product.

A few months later, the plaintiff learned that the defendant had been soliciting customers from the American customer listing and filed suit. The court noted that the list, which contained thousands of names, addresses, and phone numbers of potential customers, did possess significant value to American and to any multilevel marketing competitor that came into its possession. It was estimated that the market value of the information was approximately $150 per thousand names each time the list was utilized. Ostensibly, the defendant firm had just begun using the list, because it had contacted only as many as 50 of the names on the list and had managed to sign up only seven of those. The total dollar value of the memberships these seven customers represented to the defendant was determined to be $1,178.

Plaintiff's testimony revealed that it spent $265,000 on marketing activities during the two years previous to the contract's termination in order to compile and qualify the names on the list. Its average profit margin on the memberships it sold averaged 36 percent. The listing reportedly contained almost 28,000 names.

The United States District Court for the Eastern District of Virginia essentially was charged with assessing damages, because a summary judgment already had been entered against the defendant. The court noted that American could not recover for both a breach of contract and a misappropriation of trade secrets when the misappropriation of the trade secrets occurred under a contract provision mandating confidentiality of secrets. As an analogy, to pay for both the breach and the misappropriation in such instances would in essence be similar to paying someone twice for providing one service or product.

As the court noted, the Virginia UTSA is specific as to how damages are to be calculated, and there is sufficient case law already in existence to guide the court in deliberations pursuant to its provisions. The UTSA allows that damages can include the actual loss that was incurred from the misappropriation and any unjust enrichment caused by the misappropriation that has not already been included in the actual loss computation. Virginia's UTSA allows that, if it is impossible to prove a greater amount of damages by other methods, the damages caused by a misappropriation of trade secrets can be calculated exclusively by imposition of a reasonable royalty for a misappropriator's unauthorized use or disclosure of a trade secret. In this case, a reasonable royalty was calculated. If only the $1,178 of memberships were in question, the total damages (profits lost) would come to under $1,000. Apparently, much more was considered to have been at stake and involved in this misappropriation, and that is the reason the court deemed it necessary to impose a reasonable royalty.

The royalty imposed by the court was calculated based on a fictional scenario developed by the court in which the defendants had "leased" the customer information from the plaintiff. Several assumptions went into this fictional leasing of names, not the least of which was the willingness of the plaintiff to lease the names to potential competitors in the first place. Obviously, leasing a customer list to a competitor is a highly unlikely event. However, the court had to devise such a fictional scenario and make other assumptions based on expert testimony in order to arrive at its royalty determination. Based on an estimated number of names leased and applying a market value to the names on the basis of the testimony presented, the court arrived at a royalty (damages) of $22,500. Further, the court noted that the $22,500 was the total award for direct damages; the $1,178 earned from the sales of the memberships was not included in the award amount because, when a royalty is calculated, it becomes the exclusive remedy available to the claimant.

As for punitive damages and attorney fees, the court awarded neither. The UTSA allows awards of punitive damages and recovery of attorney fees but only in cases involving willful and malicious misappropriation of secrets. Willful and malicious acts are those that are taken without regard to the rights of others and involve intentional infliction of ill will. The actions of the defendants may have been contemptible and were found to be illegal, but they were not viewed as being serious breaches of loyalty nor did they impose serious damage on American Sales Corporation. As a result, requests for punitive damages and attorney fees were denied.

In summary, the UTSA allows for damages, injunctive relief, and, in some cases, punitive damages and attorney fees. Punitive damages and attorney fees are recoverable in situations in which willful and malicious misappropriation of trade secrets is shown to exist. A court may impose royalties when presented with a situation in which damage calculation through other means is difficult or impossible.

Section 5. Preservation of Secrecy

In an action under this Act, a court shall preserve the secrecy of an alleged trade secret by reasonable means, which may include granting protective orders in connection with discovery proceedings, holding in-camera hearings, sealing the records of the action, and ordering any person involved in the litigation not to disclose an alleged trade secret without prior court approval.

Another crucial issue for which the act provides is the ongoing protection of a firm's trade secrets, even during legal proceedings pursuant to actions filed under the auspices of the UTSA. As can be seen in this section, a court shall preserve the secrecy of a trade secret by ordering reasonable steps pursuant to such an effort. This stipulation allows courts to compel parties involved in cases under the UTSA to maintain secrecy relative to the secrets in question. Plaintiffs who are charging misappropriation of their trade secrets undoubtedly will want to ask the courts to ensure such protection during the discovery phase of the case and subsequent formal courtroom hearings. An injunction, if successfully obtained, would entail efforts to protect trade secrets after the injunction is issued. Firms seeking recognition and protection of their trade secrets in court would be wise to seek court protection during the entire length of the proceedings; otherwise, a question may arise as to whether reasonable steps had been taken by the plaintiff to protect information the plaintiff claims is secret and valuable.

Section 6. Statute of Limitations

An action for misappropriation must be brought within 3 years after the misappropriation is discovered or by the exercise of reasonable diligence should have been discovered. For the purposes of this section, a continuing misappropriation constitutes a single claim.

A firm that finds itself the victim of a trade secrets misappropriation must seek legal protection of its secrets and damages from those responsible for the misappropriation within three years of the discovery of the misappropriation. Failure to file a charge within the three year time limit causes the firm to relinquish any rights it may have been able to pursue under the UTSA. The wording of the act purposefully specifies that charging parties must pursue their legal efforts within three years of the discovery or three years of a period of time in which the plaintiffs, using reasonable diligence, should have been expected to discover that a misappropriation of its secrets had occurred.

Further, this section of the UTSA specifies that a continuing misappropriation constitutes a single claim. For example, one may envision a situation in which a trade secret misappropriation was discovered five years prior to the filing of a suit seeking damages and an injunction. The complainant missed filing charges during the three years immediately after discovering the misappropriation. Despite an apparent failing to file on time, charges are pursued by the complainant, based on the theory that the secrets are still being misappropriated and, therefore, the filing is timely, not late. In other words, because a misappropriation occurs on what may be perceived as a daily basis, the complainant claims to meet the statute of limitations time line of three years. The courts would not buy such an argument on timeliness, because a continuing misappropriation discovered more than three years prior to filing charges is viewed as "the" misappropriation and any redress sought under the UTSA must be filed within three years of the discovery of the misappropriation.

In *Sokol Crystal Products, Inc. v. DSC Communications Corporation*, the question of timeliness with regard to the statute of limitations relative to filing charges under the UTSA was one of several areas brought into question during the proceedings. The issue of particular relevance to a discussion on the statute of limitations embodied in the act that arose in this case dealt with when, exactly, does the specified three year time limit begin. Obviously, such a determination could have profound consequences in a particular circumstance given that, if a timely suit is not filed pursuant to the three year limitation, a firm would lose its chance for remedy for a misappropriation.

Sokol Crystal Products, Inc., manufactures crystal oscillators for use in a variety of telecommunications switching devices and other electronic equipment. Crystal oscillators have at their heart a piezoelectric crystal that determines the frequency of the vibration produced by the crystal. The frequency can be controlled by a specific application of electrical current to the crystal. Sokol contracted with a firm now owned by DSC Communications to provide it with a particular type of crystal oscillator known for its extremely high frequency. DSC planned to use the crystal component in its telecommunications switching devices. Each of the devices incorporating such crystals required over 1,000 of the crystals in order to be operational

Prior to contracting with Sokol, DSC's predecessor (Granger Associates) sought to acquire high frequency crystals that would suit its needs from other outside sources but was unable to find a suitable supply.

Granger even approached one of its own subsidiaries about the possibility of it producing the crystals the parent firm required. The subsidiary reportedly balked at the suggestion, noting that such a production would be costly and infringe on the available space to an extent that might impose limitations on its operations. After the subsidiary declined the opportunity to develop and produce the crystals, Granger came upon Sokol. Sokol submitted a proposal detailing its potential to supply the high frequency crystals desired by Granger. Shortly thereafter, Granger ordered a supply of the crystals as samples. Two months later, the firms entered into a confidential information agreement with the purpose of protecting Sokol's trade secrets. In general, the agreement prohibited Granger from using Sokol's confidential information for any purpose other than the express purpose for which it was offered. Sokol began shipping crystals to Granger pursuant to its contract.

Purportedly, at about this same time, the Granger subsidiary that had balked at the prospect of developing and producing the high frequency crystals was ordered by the parent firm to develop a suitable crystal for its needs. In less than a year, the subsidiary finalized its crystal design.

The crystals being delivered by Sokol were alleged to have had a higher failure rate than desired by Granger. It was reported that Granger had its engineers examine some of the crystals with the purpose of helping Sokol produce a better product. As a part of this effort, one of Granger's engineers reverse-engineered the crystal, even to the point of making schematics of the circuit. Only 18 months after signing the confidentiality agreement, Granger cancelled the delivery of any further crystals from Sokol. Granger then began using crystals produced by its own subsidiary and also purchased some from another outside source.

Claiming that its trade secrets had been misappropriated under Wisconsin's UTSA, Sokol sued Granger's new owner, DSC. Apparently there was no direct evidence that anyone at DSC used Sokol's confidential information in the making of its own crystals, but the jury award of almost $2.5 million dollars indicated that the similarity in the crystals and the fact that DSC had access to Sokol's trade secrets during the development of its own crystals was enough for the jury to infer that a misappropriation had occurred and that Sokol had been damaged by the misappropriation. DSC appealed the decision, noting among its assertions that the suit should have been barred by the statute of limitations. Sokol cross-appealed, claiming that the jury had not been instructed as to the possibility of a willful or malicious misappropriation and, therefore, the court returned a lesser award than deemed desirable or required by Sokol.

As noted in the UTSA (and in Wisconsin's version), an action claiming misappropriation of a trade secret "shall be commenced within three years after the misappropriation of a trade secret is discovered or should have been discovered by the exercise of reasonable diligence." Sokol filed suit on November 15, 1991. Factoring in the three year time limit, a claimed misappropriation would have had to have occurred or should have been discovered by Sokol after November 15, 1988, in order for the suit to have been filed in a timely manner. If the misappropriation in question occurred prior to that date, then the suit would not have been filed in a timely manner and, therefore, could not proceed.

In trying to pin down exactly when a misappropriation occurred, it was noted that Sokol gave its trade secrets to Granger, albeit accompanied with the confidentiality agreement barring the unauthorized use of Sokol's secrets. Therefore, if a misappropriation occurred, it would have been based not on when the secrets were acquired, because they had been acquired legally, but when they had been disclosed or used contrary to the law. The court centered its focus on the date of the misuse of Sokol's secrets and the date that Sokol knew or should reasonably have known of the misuse. As was already noted, the jury inferred that a misappropriation had occurred, because of the similarity in the crystals and because Granger had access to Sokol's secrets. Because such a misuse was inferred, a specific date had not been determined as to an actual occurrence. Therefore, the most telling factor is the date that Sokol learned of the misappropriation or reasonably should have known that its secrets were being misused.

Sokol claimed that it did not learn of the misuse until after Granger began selling its switches using crystals from its own subsidiary and was able to note the similarity in the two products. Ostensibly, this was sometime after November 1988, the month the purchase contract with Sokol had been canceled and Granger moved to supply its switches with crystals from its own subsidiary. However, DSC argues that Sokol should have reasonably known of a misappropriation (assuming one occurred) in July 1988, when it showed Sokol employees examples of crystal boards from its subsidiary. Though privy to the existence of the boards and noting that the boards were similar to their own, the employees were not informed as to the intended use of the boards, and although perhaps suspicious, the employees harbored only concerns or suspicions about the boards, not knowledge of a misappropriation. Suspicions or concerns do not translate directly into knowledge of a misdeed, and in such situations, it can be argued that only knowledge is actionable.

Therefore, the clock on the statute of limitations would not have begun to run until after Sokol had a chance to assess the subsidiary's crystal and determine its similarity to its own product. In this case, such an assessment supposedly occurred after the November 1988 purchase contract cancellation. Because the suit had been filed on November 15, 1991, it was deemed to have been filed in a timely manner.

In another case in which the statute of limitations and its impact on the outcome became central to the findings, a manufacturer of heart defibrillators sued a competitor and two of its former employees, claiming they were misappropriating its secrets. In the case of *Intermedics, Inc. v. Ventritex, Inc. et al.*, two factors were seen as playing critical roles in the court's deliberations. Both were related to the statute of limitations as embodied in law. First, a decision as to when the time period under the statute began had to be made in order to recognize whether or not a timely filing had been made. In other words, the court needed to decide when the legal clock started running. Second, the question arose as to whether a recent use of a trade secret by an unauthorized individual for the benefit of another, which should have been known to the owner of the secret or should have been recognized as having been compromised years earlier, lead to the conclusion that trade secrets have been or are currently being misappropriated.

Intermedics is a manufacturer of technically complex medical devices. A major product line of the firm is composed of its implantable defibrillators. The firm considered many aspects relating to the construction and design of the devices to be among its trade secrets. Intermedics charged two former employees and their employer with misappropriation of those secrets, breach of contract, breach of fiduciary duty, and a variety of other charges.

At trial on the charges, several important factors surfaced. One of the more important factors dealt with the fact that the plaintiff had filed suit against the same defendants over four years prior to the current suit for a misappropriation of its secrets. In that case, Intermedics claimed that its former employees were bound not to disclose trade secrets of their employer and, contrary to their legal duty, disclosed its defibrillator trade secrets to Ventritex in the course of subsequent employment. In short, the earlier suit contained almost the same charges against the same parties as had been filed in the current suit. In the course of the old suit's discovery process, the defendant agreed to allow a representative of Intermedics to conduct an audit with respect to its trade secrets claim. The representative completed the audit. As a part of the audit, the auditor compared a list of alleged secrets submitted by Intermedics with the findings of an on-site visit. Subsequently, the plaintiff dropped its first lawsuit filed against the defendants.

Some four years later, the current charges were filed. The similarity to the charges filed in the first action was not lost on the court. The outcome of the suit hinged on whether or not trade secrets existed and had been misappropriated and, given that such had occurred, whether or not the current action had been filed in a timely manner. The charges in this case alleged that 37 trade secrets related to the heart defibrillators had been misappropriated.

The court recognized that the issues surrounding the 37 alleged trade secrets were quite complex and technical in nature. As such, it recognized that a jury would be placed in an extremely intimidating and uncomfortable situation relative to understanding and comprehending the technologies and associated vocabularies involved. As a result, the court ordered that a multistage trial process be implemented in which the first trial would be limited to the determination of liability, not damages, with respect to a limited number of the secrets. At the direction of the court, the plaintiff selected 4 of the 37 alleged secrets and the defendant selected 2 others that served as the basis for the trial.

The jury made several findings of fact relative to the charges. Among these findings was that the fact that the auditor who had conducted the first trade secrets audit of Ventritex years earlier had done so as an agent of the plaintiff. The jury did not find that the information in dispute was a trade secret at the time the employees worked for the plaintiff. Related to the trade secrets question, the jury noted that the design ideas claimed to be secret were, in fact, disclosed in documents that had been made available to the auditor in the earlier suit. It was noted that these same documents were available to the plaintiff and its legal counsel.

As a matter of deliberation, the court considered the question of the statute of limitations pertaining to the charges involving misappropriation of trade secrets that the defendants claimed should have expired prior to the filing of this suit. The U.S. District Court for the Northern District of California considered the question of the statute of limitations. Given the variety of charges, the longest statute of limitation that would have a bearing on any of the charges as stated in the suit (other than civil conspiracy, which was to be tried separately) was four years. The court noted that state law (the UTSA) provides a three year statute of limitation governing trade secrets misappropriation. Given that the jury found all of the design secrets had been included in the documents made available to the plaintiff's auditor and were placed at the disposal of or were discoverable to the plaintiff and its counsel in the earlier suit, and given that claims related to these six designs did not arise, the conclusion that they did not constitute the plaintiff's secrets at the time appears reasonable. That the earlier suit should have included these designs in its claims had they been a secret stood as a reasonable foundation to find that the statute of limitations had begun to run prior to the dismissal of the earlier suit. In effect, the jury felt that, if the designs were secret, the plaintiff could have discovered with reasonable diligence that the designs had been misappropriated. Because the earlier suit had been dismissed over four years previously, the statute of limitations relative to the claims at issue here had run its course.

The UTSA specifies that actions arising from a misappropriation need to commence within three years of the discovery of the misappropriation or within three years of when the misappropriation should have been discovered using reasonable diligence. The courts enforce the statute of limitation provision in the act. One other important point that the court made in the *Intermedics* case was that the circumstances of each case need to be taken into account in deliberating the issues raised. Seldom are the circumstances that give rise to legal suits exactly alike. In this case, the allegations that the former employees had taken its secrets at the same time, from the same place, for the same commercial purpose for a known competitor, that the secrets were related to one, highly technical product where there is knowledge that some design aspects have been misappropriated all lead to the conclusion that, if some of the design aspects of the secrets were compromised, one would expect that all of the secrets in the design had been compromised. As such, the earlier suit should have included in its charges the misappropriation of these aspects of the product design if it had expectations of recovering for their misuse.

Section 7. Effect on Other Law

(a) *This act displaces conflicting tort, restitutionary, and other law of this State pertaining to civil liability for misappropriation of a trade secret.*

(b) *This act does not affect:*
   (1) *contractual or other civil liability or relief that is not based upon misappropriation of a trade secret; or*
   (2) *criminal liability for misappropriation of a trade secret.*

Section 7 deals with the notion that, on the effective date of the UTSA within the jurisdiction, the act takes precedent over other tort, restitutionary, and other laws relevant to a civil liability arising from the misappropriation of a trade secret. It replaces the adopting state's previous laws dealing with the misappropriation of a trade secret. In addition, this section clearly delineates its bounds by stating that it does not affect either contractual or civil liability beyond the scope of a trade secret misappropriation nor does it affect any criminal liability that may arise because of the misappropriation of a trade secret.

A relevant case witnessed the purported developer and inventor of a screw-based auger system designed to move petroleum-based drilling mud from drilling platforms on offshore oil rigs to storage tanks, which facilitated the movement of the mud to barges for transport to landfills for disposal, sue a major oil company for unjust enrichment. The case, *McPhearson v. Shell Oil Company et al.*, focused on whether there were other remedies available to the plaintiff (McPhearson) for the alleged unjust enrichment. There were. Louisiana had adopted the UTSA in 1981, approximately ten years prior to the actions that led to the charges being filed, and as is detailed in the act, the UTSA takes precedent over other potential civil liabilities arising from an alleged misappropriation of trade secrets.

McPhearson had been employed as a welder on an offshore oil rig located in the Gulf of Mexico. As a consequence of using petroleum-based drilling mud, his firm was required to capture and safely dispose of the mud on land. In drilling wells, companies sometimes can choose between petroleum-based muds and water-based drilling muds. Water-based drilling muds are preferred as to their disposal, because they can be dumped into the gulf or other bodies of water without significant concern for the environment. However, petroleum-based muds are superior in certain drilling situations and, as a result, often are used where water-based muds would be deemed deficient. Drilling with petroleum-based mud creates extra headaches for those so engaged, because the mud must be stored until it can be off-loaded for transport to land. When the mud is moved to the transport tanks, it is allowed to pour into troughs that direct the flow into the storage tanks. Gravity does the work of moving the mud along the trough. Unfortunately, the operation of moving the mud via the troughs is fraught with environmental hazards, because spills or splashes occur, causing some of the mud to fall onto the floors of the rigs (causing safety concerns) and, potentially, into the Gulf (creating environmental concerns). This method also requires extra employee vigilance, because clogs or obstructions periodically occur, creating work stoppages and potential spills. When obstructions occur, employees on the rig rely on the use of paddles and shovels to clear the obstruction in order to get the mud flow moving again. It is time-consuming and labor intensive and, as a result, can be a relatively expensive procedure.

That is where McPhearson stepped in. While employed on a rig, he reportedly approached his supervisor about the possibility of his developing an enclosed pipe auger system that would use mechanical energy in lieu of gravity to move the mud. The auger would eliminate the rig's reliance on gravity to do a job that might best be done with mechanical energy. The auger was envisioned as a way of minimizing the risk of clogs or obstructions, because the screw action of the auger would push through obstructions without the intervention of human help. He explained his idea first to his foreman and later to other employees of his drilling company and a representative of Shell Oil Company. It was purported that the Shell representative encouraged him to build the system if he felt it would be an improvement over the trough system. After receiving a list of materials needed, the Shell employee ordered and had delivered the materials McPhearson needed. The plaintiff constructed the system with the help of other employees on the rig. The system used a large auger to move the materials inside a closed pipe and, as envisioned, reduced the need for human intervention and the potential for unwanted, potentially harmful spills. The system was singularly praised for its effectiveness by those privy to its operations.

McPhearson recognized that the system might have commercial possibilities and decided to look into building such systems and leasing them to Shell and other firms that required moving environmentally hazardous drilling mud. It was reported that, after returning to land, McPhearson met with a representative of Shell in New Orleans who was familiar with the success of the system. The representative supposedly mentioned that everyone who had heard of the system's effectiveness was enthused about it. The Shell employee and McPhearson were said to have agreed to another meeting later in the week, ostensibly for investigating the possibility of McPhearson producing auger systems on a large scale and, in turn, leasing them to Shell.

At the second meeting, McPhearson reportedly discussed his producing and leasing the systems to Shell. The rental was pegged initially at $250 per day. The Shell employee allegedly stated that he would authorize the purchase of the materials needed by McPhearson to build the systems. According to the plaintiff, he and the employee shook hands to seal the deal.

On his return to the rig, McPhearson was surprised to learn that he had been fired by the drilling company. The auger system continued to be used on the rig. The plaintiff acknowledged that, by the time he had been terminated, the system had been inspected by various members of the drilling industry, some of whom had taken photographs of the system. The plaintiff had made no effort to maintain the secrecy of the system, nor had he applied for a patent on the system.

Subsequently, McPhearson sued Shell and other relevant individuals in an effort to recover damages for unjust enrichment caused by their continuing to use his auger-based system for moving the mud. The Civil District Court's judgment in favor of McPhearson was overturned by the Court of Appeal for the Fourth Circuit of Louisiana. In order to recover for unjust enrichment, a plaintiff must show that the defendant (Shell et al.) has been enriched, that the plaintiff has been impoverished as a result of the enrichment, that there was no justification for the impoverishment or enrichment, and that the plaintiff had no other remedy at law, and that is where the UTSA had a major bearing on McPhearson's suit.

The Court of Appeal noted that the UTSA specifically allows owners of trade secrets the ability to obtain injunctive relief and damages arising from a misappropriation. As stated in the definition, the UTSA "displaces conflicting tort, restitutionary, and other law of this state pertaining to civil liability for misappropriation of a trade secret." This part of the act is specific in its delineation that remedies for the misappropriation of trade secrets need to be pursued under the auspices of the UTSA. As a result, the Supreme Court found that the trial court erred in finding that no legal remedy was available to the plaintiff, and, thus, the judgment in favor of the plaintiff for unjust enrichment was overturned. The plaintiff should have pursued his rights relative to the misappropriation of trade secrets under the provisions of the UTSA.

However, the high court's decision implied that, had McPhearson's claims been based on a trade secrets misappropriation per se, he would still have had trouble, because it was doubtful that the system constituted a trade secret under the law. Specifically, he had allowed others in the industry to view and photograph the device. Several individuals had helped him construct the device, none of whom were under a confidentiality agreement with the plaintiff. McPhearson had made no attempt to conceal the system from the public. It was being used on the rig in plain sight of visitors and employees with no restrictions of any kind, and no instructions to maintain secrecy were in effect. The system was not a secret by the time the plaintiff had decided to pursue legal recourse for its use. The Supreme Court noted that the "inventor" did not avail himself of the protection offered by the UTSA. As a result, the court noted that any unjust enrichment was because of the plaintiff not protecting his system and preventing it from entering the public domain. The plaintiff failed to avail himself of the benefits of the UTSA. Instead, he sued for unjust enrichment. Because the UTSA displaces other law relevant to a trade secrets misappropriation, the UTSA would have been the proper avenue for the plaintiff to have sought remedy if he had kept secret his system and had implemented reasonable efforts under the circumstances to maintain that secrecy.

The UTSA provides for the protection of trade secrets in those jurisdictions that have adopted the act. In short, there was a legal remedy available under the UTSA. The court noted that McPhearson waived his remedy by placing his secrets in the public domain. Because the UTSA was the prevailing law and because the plaintiff's actions or lack of action in effect waived his rights under the UTSA, the Supreme Court reversed the trial court's finding and dismissed the suit at cost to the plaintiff.

Another relevant case revolved around whether an association's code of conduct that specifies that disputes between members will be arbitrated can be enforced in situations in which trade secrets and other proprietary property rights are in dispute. The case, *McMahan Securities Co. L.P. v. Forum Capital Markets L.P. et al.*, involved individuals and firms in the securities industry and centered around a trade secrets dispute. Complicating the matter somewhat was the fact that the individuals and firms involved were members of the National Association of Securities Dealers (NASD). Further complicating the situation was the effect that the Federal Arbitration Act had on the expectations and actions of those involved. Under the Federal Arbitration Act, a district court is obligated to stay or refrain from court proceedings in cases in which the parties have agreed in writing to arbitrate an issue or issues. The federal act leaves no discretion with the district court in such matters. An agreement to arbitrate disputes is an agreement in its simplest form and must be honored by the courts in disputes arising under the auspices of any binding arbitration agreement as entered into by the parties.

McMahan Securities Company charged Forum Capital Markets and its principals with several federal and state violations, including the misappropriation of trade secrets involving a computer system designed to handle complex securities trading. Additionally, Forum was charged with the theft of various other types of information the plaintiff firm considered to be among its trade secrets, including its client lists, various research reports, reports of past investment performances of various securities tracked by the firm, and other proprietary material that the plaintiff claimed was its own.

The suit was filed despite the parties being potentially bound to the NASD Code of Arbitration, which mandates arbitration of disputes, claims, or controversies arising out of or in connection with the business of its members. The code does allow for some specific exceptions.

McMahan's claim that the dispute was an employee dispute, thus, beyond the scope of the NASD Code, was agreed to by the district judge. However, the U.S. Court of Appeals disagreed and sent the case back to the district court with instructions to order arbitration.

McMahan's argument that the dispute was an employment dispute and, thus, not subject to arbitration did not appear to be received well by the appeals court, nor was the contention that copyright disputes were an unsuitable subject or domain for arbitration. The appeals court cited a U.S. Supreme Court directive concerning arbitration of disputes that states that "doubts concerning the scope of arbitrable issues should be resolved in favor of arbitration." The fact that a clear code of conduct existed through which members of the association were obligated to arbitrate disputes played a major role in the court's decision to send the matter to arbitration.

Thus, the existence and implementation of the UTSA does not override the existence of a legal, contractual agreement. Parties to agreements, to arbitrate copyright disputes, for instance, are not relieved from their obligation to arbitrate disputes merely because of the adoption of the UTSA by a particular state and the fact that trade secrets allegedly are involved. Indeed, in this section of the definition, it can be inferred that the UTSA is not meant to override or remove any obligation assumed under a good faith contract, including agreements to arbitrate disputes involving trade secrets.

Section 8. Uniformity of Application and Construction

This Act shall be applied and construed to effectuate its general purpose to make uniform the law with respect to the subject of this Act among states enacting it.

This section of the act states that it is the purpose of the adopting state to make uniform the law and its impact among the adopting states' laws concerning trade secrets. As one would expect, Section 8 is an important factor in the effort to have a uniform law on which businesses everywhere can depend for protection of their proprietary secrets.

Uniformity in the application of trade secrets law has been desired by many for a long time. Differences between various states' statutes in the past made it very difficult for firms operating in multistate locations to pursue their proprietary property rights effectively. Strategic planning to protect trade secrets is impeded in an environment devoid of consistency in the law. This section of the UTSA merely acknowledges that, in adopting the act, the various state legislatures acknowledge that it is their intent that trade secrets law be effectively implemented and consistently administered.

Section 9. Short Title

This Act may be cited as the Uniform Trade Secrets Act.

In legal matters, the courts, their officers, attorneys, and others involved in administering the law can refer to the act as the UTSA. This allows those involved in legal challenges relative to trade secrets the benefit of an easy citation and improved consistency in their efforts pursuant to trade secrets legislation.

Section 10. Severability

If any provision of this Act or its application to any person or circumstances is held invalid, the invalidity does not affect other provisions or applications of the Act which can be given effect without the invalid provision or application, and to this end the provisions of this Act are severable.

This section includes a statement that is similar to those found in most commercial legislation enacted in recent years. The idea of severability is to prevent an otherwise valid case from being impeded or not proceeding on the grounds that a part of the act as adopted was declared unconstitutional or otherwise invalid within the adopting jurisdiction. By including this section, the adopting legislatures acknowledge that providing trade secrets protection is important enough that, should a part of the act be declared invalid, businesses still can avail themselves of the remainder of the act, given that the remainder stands free of any declared invalidity. Including such a statement in proposed legislation of all kinds and in contracts between businesses has become standard operating procedure in current legislative efforts and business contracting.

Section 11. Time of Taking Effect

This Act takes effect on _____, and does not apply to misappropriation occurring prior to the effective date.

Obviously, the act, once adopted, must take effect on a specific date. This section is standard fare as well, stating the date that the act becomes effective and that it applies to misappropriations occurring after the effective date. As one would expect, the date of the effective enactment of the act varies among the states adopting the act. Currently, 40 states and the District of Columbia have adopted the UTSA. By the time you read this, others may have adopted the act.

Section 12. Repeal

The following Acts and parts of Acts are repealed:

This section of the act merely points out that other state laws concerning trade secrets misappropriation no longer are considered in effect once the UTSA has been implemented.

That is it. A relatively straightforward embodiment of the need to provide for the protection of proprietary information (trade secrets) under state law. The UTSA defines trades secrets, expects reasonable efforts to be expended in providing for the protection and continued secrecy of the information, and allows for protection and recompense in the event that a firm's trade secrets are misappropriated.

Still, as straightforward as the law is and as specific as its details are, there remains the fact that firms still are finding themselves victims of trade secrets misappropriation. There have been numerous suits filed in the past ten years seeking court protection and recompense for misappropriation of trade secrets. In many instances, firms failed to garner the protection and remedies they sought because of oversights on the part of executives or a less than thorough understanding of the act and its interpretation as clarified through case law.

To avail oneself of the protection offered through the UTSA, one needs to understand the act, have a knowledge and understanding of the many cases that have delineated the scope of the act and the expectations of the court relative to the act, and be in a position in conjunction with competent legal counsel to implement a management strategy based on such knowledge. The act does not expect the impossible from executives to whom trade secrets are entrusted, only that they will expend reasonable efforts to recognize and maintain secrecy surrounding their trade secrets. The expectation that reasonableness changes given the circumstances of each case is realistic and needs to be noted by executives. Efforts perceived as reasonable in one work environment may be viewed as lax elsewhere, with dire consequences.

The following chapters provide an overview of the efforts an executive needs to pursue to adequately provide for and seek protection of a firm's trade secrets. In each chapter, summaries and explanations of legal cases that have made it through the courts are detailed to emphasize and explain the importance of specific actions necessary to fully avail oneself of the protection provided through the UTSA. The cases and their findings are not provided so that executives will become legal experts; they are provided so that executives can gain insight into the necessity of taking strategic steps to adequately protect their secrets and to give them enough information to enable them to conduct intelligent conversations and inquiries into their own firm's efforts at protecting trade secrets.

Indeed, as will be seen later, it is of paramount importance that executives obtain competent legal counsel when preparing a plan of action aimed at protecting their proprietary property rights as granted through trade secrets law. The importance of establishing and maintaining an atmosphere of confidentiality, recognizing the value of the information for which protection is desired, being specific as to which information the firm will expend efforts to protect, and encompassing one's efforts in a strategic plan aimed at recognizing and protecting a firm's trade secrets cannot be overemphasized. Competent legal counsel can and should play an important role in the development of an effective plan of action.

SUMMARY OF CONCEPTS

1. A trade secret must be secret information in that it must not be known to or readily knowable by others who could make use of the information.

2. Trade secrets must possess significant value.

3. Trade secrets must be the subject of reasonable efforts to maintain secrecy given the circumstances.

4. The UTSA provides for the security of secrets during legal proceedings.

5. The UTSA provides for the recovery of damages for secrets misappropriation.

6. Punitive damages and attorney fees are recoverable in situations involving willful and malicious misappropriations.

7. In cases involving allegations of trade secrets misappropriation, the UTSA and its provisions take precedent over other state law.

APPENDIX: CITATIONS AND
MANAGEMENT IMPLICATIONS

Corrosion Specialties and Supply, Inc., v. Dicharry et al. 631 So.2d 1389 (La.App. 5 Cir. 1994) — Information must not be generally known to others who can benefit from its knowledge or readily ascertainable by others to qualify as a trade secret.

Imed Corporation et al. v. Systems Engineering Associates et al. 602 So.2d 344 (Ala. 1992) — A user or discloser of misappropriated trade secrets can be liable if the user knew or should have known of the misappropriation. The source of the notice is not germane so long as the notice is sufficient to alert the user.

205 Corporation v. Brandow et al. 517 N.W.2d 548 (Iowa 1994) — Secret information that possesses value, that is subject to reasonable efforts under the circumstances to maintain secrecy, and that possesses independent value qualifies as a trade secret. Food recipes can be a trade secret. What is "reasonable under the circumstances" changes from environment to environment.

Capital Tool and Manufacturing Company, Inc. v. Maschinenfabrik Herkules et al. 837 F.2d 171 (4th Cir. 1988) — The purpose of a preliminary injunction is to preserve the relative positions of the parties involved until a trial on the merits can be held. The court will use its discretion given the circumstances in deciding requests for injunctions. The UTSA does not mandate that a court issue an injunction.

Ackerman v. Kimball International, Inc. 634 N.E.2d 778 (Ind.App. 1 Dist. 1994) — Threatened misappropriations may be enjoined. Misuse does not have to have taken place in order for the UTSA to apply.

Centrol, Inc., v. Morrow et. al. 489 N.W.2d 890 (S.D. 1992) — In cases in which willful and malicious misappropriation is found to occur, attorney fees may be awarded. Covenants not to compete need to be legal as to time and place.

American Sales Corporation v. Adventure Travel, Inc. 862 F.Supp. 1476 (E.D.Va. 1994) — Firms potentially can recover compensatory damages, punitive damages, and attorney fees for misappropriation of secrets. However, for punitive damages and attorney fees, a willful and malicious misappropriation must have occurred.

Sokol Crystal Products, Inc. v. DSC Communications Corporation 15 F.3d 1427 (7th Cir. 1994) — The UTSA allows for a three year statute of limitations during which suits must be filed to be timely. The clock begins to run when one discovers or reasonably should have discovered that a misappropriation has occurred.

Intermedics, Inc. v. Ventritex, Inc. et al. 822 F.Supp. 634 (N.D.Cal. 1993) — The statute of limitations begins to run when a misappropriation is discovered or through reasonable diligence should have been discovered. A continuing misappropriation constitutes a single misappropriation.

McPhearson v. Shell Oil Company et al. 584 So.2d 373 (La.App. 4 Cir. 1991) — The UTSA prevails in cases alleging misappropriation of trade secrets. Specifically, the UTSA displaces conflicting tort, restitutionary, and other civil liability laws in situations involving trade secrets misappropriation.

McMahan Securities Co. L.P. v. Forum Capital Markets L.P. et al. 35 F.3d 82 (2nd Cir. 1994) — Agreements to arbitrate disputes are expected to be enforced. The UTSA does not relieve valid contractual obligations.

ACKNOWLEDGMENT

The text of the Uniform Trade Secrets Act is included with permission of the National Conference of Commissioners on Uniform State Laws.

3

Establishing a Climate of Confidentiality

In considering the definition of "trade secret" as provided in the Uniform Trade Secrets Act (UTSA), one notes that there is the expectation that such a secret will be the "subject of efforts that are reasonable under the circumstances to maintain its secrecy." Reasonableness varies according to the circumstances and, perhaps, according to the value of the information in a given environment. However, executives need to be aware that there is an expectation that secrets will be subject to efforts to protect those secrets. In pursuing such an effort, executives will need to be aware of several avenues that are worth consideration.

First, executives need to be concerned with the creation of an atmosphere of confidentiality regarding their trade secrets. This pursuit alone may require a variety of efforts, none of which by themselves may qualify as a reasonable effort but when taken as a whole will indicate that a firm is taking constructive steps to protect its proprietary property.

Providing folders stamped "confidential — not for disclosure" for the storing of any information deemed a secret would be a cheap and easy start toward providing for an atmosphere of confidentiality surrounding a firm's secrets. Requiring prospective employees and current employees to sign an agreement recognizing the confidentiality, value, and ownership of the information deemed to be a secret of a firm would add to the climate desired. Using lockable file cabinets that are secured when they contain information pertaining to a firm's secrets, using private codes to gain access to computerized files, fully destroying records instead of throwing them away, and other security measures all can add to the atmosphere of confidentiality that a business executive would desire for the protection of his or her firm's trade secrets.

Firms that have developed such an atmosphere have found that such an effort goes a long way in establishing the concept that the firm has secrets that are valued and that its management takes seriously its responsibility to provide for their security. It is of interest that, in many of the cases that have progressed through the courts, confidentiality and reasonableness with regard to secrecy maintenance efforts are often at the center of the court's decision as to whether a firm prevails in its legal efforts to show misappropriation or whether the firm loses in such efforts.

CONFIDENTIALITY AGREEMENTS

In *ITT Telecom Products Corporation v. Dooley*, the plaintiff sought damages it claimed occurred from the willful reporting of trade secret information to a firm that hired Dooley as a consultant in a nonrelated case against ITT. Dooley was a former employee of ITT Telecom who had ample access to the information while under the employ of that firm. The appeal court found for ITT Telecom, noting that the willful disclosure of trade secrets in violation of a contract of confidentiality does not give rise to the statutory privilege normally afforded individuals for statements made in judicial proceedings. The climate of confidentiality that existed at ITT Telecom, assisted in part by the existence of a contract of confidentiality, helped ITT pursue its legal rights and protection of its trade secrets. In other words, even though Dooley was testifying on behalf of another firm in a legal proceeding, the contract of confidentiality concerning trade secrets he had signed as an employee at ITT Telecom was still enforceable. The contention that Dooley's testimony was proper and privileged given the circumstances did not stand. Dooley's actions as a consultant and the corresponding disclosure of ITT Telecom's trade secrets were found to be in violation of ITT Telecom's proprietary property rights.

Questions concerning trade secrets misappropriation and a potential breach of a confidentiality agreement were among the issues raised in the case of *Machen, Inc. v. Aircraft Design, Inc. et al.* Machen, Inc., is engaged in the marketing of new aircraft parts in the aftermarket products business. As is seen in numerous cases involving allegations of trade secrets misappropriation, the plaintiff firm in this case charged a former employee with a misappropriation of its secrets. At the same time, it also claimed the employee violated a confidentiality agreement entered into during the course of his previous employment. It was reported that a former coordinator of research and development for Machen (and its successor firm) left his position at Machen and, in conjunction with one of the firm's former customers, started Aircraft Design, Inc. Subsequently, Aircraft Design became the exclusive distributor of a modified braking system that could be utilized on a particular line of private aircraft, ostensibly to improve the braking ability of such aircraft. The braking system was manufactured by a third party, Cleveland Brake.

Shortly after Aircraft Design's entrance into the aircraft brake business, Machen filed suit against Aircraft Design and its owners, claiming to own the trade secrets inherent in the new brake system and charging misappropriation of secrets related to that system and to other proprietary information as it related to perceived shortcomings in the original equipment brakes. Prior to going to court, the suit was amended and countercharges leveled. A major addition to the suit was a further claim that the defendants had misappropriated other trade secrets related to an engine modification project undertaken by Machen. At the trial, Machen's claims for trade secrets misappropriation and breach of contract claims were dismissed.

As a means of reviewing the decision's impact on strategic management efforts, several background factors as noted in the record need to be brought to light, because they bear on the decision. First, Machen claimed that the brake system modification was a trade secret belonging to it. By definition, a trade secret is information that derives independent economic value from not being generally known to, or being readily ascertainable by proper means by, other persons who can obtain economic advantage from its disclosure or use and that is the subject of efforts that are reasonable under the circumstances to maintain its secrecy. In a claim of trade secrets misappropriation, the plaintiff (charging party) bears the burden of showing that legally protectable trade secrets exist and that such were misappropriated. If legally protectable secrets do not exist, then there can be no misappropriation. Delving into the background information surrounding the case adds to the understanding that led to the decision not supporting Machen's charges of misappropriation.

In responding to the charge of trade secrets misappropriation, the defendant argued that the information was not a secret because he purportedly had conceived the brake system modifications prior to his employment with Machen. Affidavits and depositions with former colleagues and acquaintances made prior to the defendant's employment with Machen were submitted in support of his stance. Further, the defendant claimed that information related to any perceived deficiency in the original equipment brakes was not a secret, because the strengths and limitations of the original equipment brakes were well-known in the industry. Pilots, mechanics, and others familiar with the plane's capabilities were purportedly all in positions of knowing or being able to readily ascertain that deficiencies in the braking system existed. The defendant claimed he was just one of many in the industry who was aware of the brake deficiency, he had knowledge of the deficiency prior to accepting employment at Machen, and, as a result, the knowledge could not be a trade secret belonging to Machen.

A third-party brake on which the modification was based also was proffered as not constituting a trade secret, because anyone viewing the modification could ascertain readily, using proper means, the method by which the modification had been accomplished. It was argued that, because any secret inherent in the modification was readily observable by anyone viewing the braking system, it could not meet the criteria that trade secrets be comprised of information that is secret and not readily ascertainable by others. In short, it could be argued that reverse-engineering the modifications would be a relatively straightforward process, thus, negating the secrecy expectation.

Another factor that potentially bore on the decision as to whether a trade secret existed was the revelation that an employee of the plaintiff had discussed with Cleveland Brake representatives the possibility of Cleveland making such a brake for the plaintiff. The discussion supposedly took place at a trade show. Cleveland's employee apparently was not asked to sign a confidentiality agreement as a condition of the discussion, nor did the employee enter into any express agreement not to disclose or use the information discussed.

The UTSA expects that efforts to maintain secrecy that are reasonable under the circumstances will be made by those responsible for the secret. Reasonable under the circumstances is a key concept that arises in many legal matters. Efforts that are deemed reasonable for certain types of information with moderate value may not be deemed reasonable for those with extremely high value. The type of business, the form of the information, specific policy expectations, and other matters all may impact the concept of reasonableness. In any case, the use of confidentiality agreements and restrictions on access are basic expectations relative to securing secrets in many business environments. In the absence of any express agreement not to disclose a secret, expectations of secrecy are unwarranted. Given that the plaintiff's employee voluntarily discussed the information with a third party while that individual was under no obligation to maintain confidentiality removes any veil of secrecy that might have existed prior to the release of the information. An argument that it was general practice in the industry to maintain one another's secrets when so divulged did not suffice. Despite providing what might have been a reasonable level of security at its place of business relative to its trade secrets, Machen's lack of preventing trade secrets disclosure at a trade show weakens any argument that reasonable steps had been taken to prevent disclosure, given the circumstances. Accordingly, the information could not be construed to be a trade secret under the UTSA.

In another vein, it is possible that, even if one considers each of the individual components of a secret as not being secret, taken as a whole, the information could be construed to be a secret. This was not one of those instances. In other words, it is possible that combinations of information that are not secret but whose specific combination or formula results in a new insight or solution that is itself not readily ascertainable, has independent economic value, and for which reasonable efforts are taken to insure and maintain its secrecy potentially could, in the specific combination as described, be delineated as a trade secret. However, in this instance, the court did not find the existence of any trade secret. Because a trade secret was not shown to exist, it stands to reason that a misappropriation could not occur. The court of appeal upheld the summary judgment of the trial court, which dismissed Machen's trade secrets claim.

The discussion or revelation of potential trade secrets at a trade show, in the absence of any security to maintain secrecy, may cause the loss of a trade secret designation for that information. Firms participating in trade shows need to take precautions not to disclose trade secrets in such public settings. Once disclosed, any potential secret loses its secrecy. Firms participating in trade shows and other public displays of products need to have their employees remain vigilant about the need to protect trade secrets. As many who participate in such shows can attest, trade shows are great places to gather and share information concerning recent developments and breakthroughs in an industry. Responsible executives will want to make sure that the information shared in public trade shows can be construed to be public information only and not information that may compromise their firm's proprietary property rights as offered under the UTSA.

Related to such an effort is the need for firms to establish policies related to the dissemination (or, rather, lack of dissemination) of potentially sensitive information. Firms that encourage employees to give public speeches, write articles, or otherwise provide information to public forums about their commercial efforts need to be sensitive to the communication needs of their employees while insuring the maintenance of their trade secrets. It is common for many large firms to place the responsibility on public relations employees to review speeches and articles written by employees who are privy to their firms' secrets with a view to preventing unwitting disclosure of proprietary information.

Although such efforts have at their heart the prevention of a potentially costly leak, they sometimes meet with distrust and agitation by employees so impacted. It is important that employees understand that such scrutiny has as its basis the maintenance of a potentially valuable competitive stance and that such scrutiny does not serve as a sweeping form of communications restraint or interference with their rights of free speech. However, despite the existence at many large firms of individuals charged with reviewing speeches and articles, most firms cannot afford a staff to provide the kind of scrutiny that some cautious executives may desire. In those situations, the necessity of implementing a specific policy statement reminding employees to remain vigilant in their public communications in order to protect the firm's secrets becomes apparent. Suffice it to say that, if a knowledgeable employee has an article published detailing a trade secret, the secret will cease to exist, as will any legal protection to which the firm or owner may have been entitled under trade secrets law.

Confidentiality agreements often are utilized as one means of assuring the security of trade secrets. Indeed, their existence and use is a normal practice in many firms, which have taken positive steps to assure the continued security of their secrets. A properly prepared and carefully worded confidentiality agreement that is understood and agreed to by employees not only serves as a legal exhibit that sometimes bolsters a charge of misappropriation but also, perhaps more importantly, gives notice to employees that the firm has information that is deemed a proprietary property of the firm and that employees are expected to respect the rights that accompany the access and use of such property. Confidentiality agreements that are worded in such a manner as to be legally enforceable should play an essential role in efforts to maintain secrecy surrounding one's trade secrets.

In *Machen*, a breach of a confidentiality agreement was charged. The trial court dismissed the claim against the former employee. In the appeal, Machen claimed that the agreement was signed by the former employee, that signing it was a condition of continuing the employment as provided, that significant training was provided to the employee as a result, and that the employee was given new responsibilities and access to additional secrets after signing the agreement. The major issues as asserted by Machen were whether or not there was adequate consideration involved to bind the parties and, as a related matter, whether or not the agreement was legally enforceable and binding to the former employee.

The defendant denied signing any confidentiality agreement. He argued that, had he signed such an agreement, signing would have occurred after he left the employ of Machen and became employed by its successor; therefore, he could not have broken an agreement with Machen. Additionally, the claim that the defendant received training as a result of signing an agreement was denied. He denied receiving access to additional secrets as claimed by the plaintiff. Further, had he signed such an agreement, he postured that his continued employment was insufficient consideration for any contract entered into after he was employed.

In reviewing the merits of the claim that a breach of a confidentiality agreement had occurred, the court noted the differences in the use of the terms "sufficiency" and "adequacy" with regard to binding parties to a contract. As the court noted, the two terms are not synonymous. If one is discussing adequacy, then a comparison of the value of promises involved in the exchange inherent in the contractual process ensues. The question of parity as it arises in a discussion related to adequacy seldom becomes the subject of a case involving breach of contract. The question of sufficiency does arise, and it does so often. Sufficiency does not concern itself with parity in the promises exchanged, only that something exists that supports the promise.

With the case at hand, the court of appeals noted that the promise of continued employment usually was sufficient to bind parties to a confidentiality agreement. It was reported that there was substantial evidence at the trial court that supported Machen's assertion that the defendant had received substantial training and experience while employed by Machen's successor. Given the promise of continued employment and the advanced training that followed, a finding that sufficient consideration existed to bind the parties to the agreement would not be surprising. However, the court noted that the agreement was not with Machen but with its successor and that the information in dispute predated the existence of the successor firm.

Despite the conclusion that confidentiality agreements normally are binding as long as sufficient consideration in the form of continued employment opportunity exists, such was not enough to bring about a conclusion to support Machen's charge. In Washington, where the trial took place, state law mandates that, in instances in which confidentiality agreements are utilized, the employer must provide in writing to the employee a notification that, among other things, specifies that the agreement does not apply to inventions for which no company facilities, equipment, supplies, or trade secrets of the employer were used. It was reported that no such written notification was issued to employees as required by the statute. Additionally, the language of the agreement contained a provision that seemed to contradict the provisions of the Washington statute covering confidentiality agreements. As the court noted, contracts that conflict with the terms of legislative enactments are illegal and unenforceable. Further, many contracts include a severability clause that protects the agreement should any part of it be declared illegal. The agreement in question did not contain a severability clause. As a result, the entire agreement as written was found to be unenforceable as a matter of law. The court of appeals upheld the trial court's dismissal of Machen's claim for breach of the confidentiality agreement.

In summary, it is necessary that reasonable steps be taken to insure that secrecy of trade secrets be maintained. The incorporation of a legally binding confidentiality agreement should be among these steps. Because matters of contract law are embedded in state law, a contract that is construed to be legal in one state may not be legal in another. The fact that Machen's confidentiality agreement was not enforceable reinforces the concept that one should take care in preparing such agreements. The necessity for obtaining competent legal counsel to assist in the preparation of confidentiality agreements is paramount. Competent legal counsel can help assure that a confidentiality agreement as incorporated in a strategic protection plan will be enforceable. Additionally, because state laws change over time, it is a good practice to have legal counsel review one's confidentiality agreements as well as one's entire protection plan on a periodic basis to assure that they continue to meet the expectations of newly enacted state legislation.

Another thought for consideration that *Machen* brings to light is the potential for the loss of trade secrets by employees who reveal secrets in conversations or other communication efforts with third parties. For instance, public involvement policies in existence at many firms encourage executives and other employees to participate in organized efforts to improve their communities. Among such community-oriented activities may be the delivery of speeches or authoring of articles related to the firm's activities that impact the economic viability of the area. A firm that is concerned with the protection of its trade secrets would do well to remind its executives and others who may be called upon to deliver formal communications that it is essential that such public communications not include information that may divulge or otherwise injure the firm's trade secrets.

A case was pursued in Florida that claimed a former employee of a nursery had gone to work for a competitor in violation of a noncompete agreement entered into between the former employee and the plaintiff firm. As a related matter that bears on trade secrets law, the former employer sought to restrain the former employee from making use, at his new place of employment, of information the employer claimed constituted a trade secret of the firm. *Lovell Farms, Inc. v. Levy* involved a nursery that claimed it owned trade secrets that comprised specialized knowledge and information relative to the growing of plants. It charged that its former employee was using its secrets in competition with it in violation of an explicit noncompete covenant.

Levy, the former employee, was a horticulturist. He was reported to have entered into a noncompete agreement with Lovell during the course of his employment with that firm. The agreement stipulated that the employee would not compete with Lovell in an area comprising southern Florida for a period of five years should he leave the employ of Lovell. There was disagreement as to whether Levy voluntarily quit Lovell's employ or was discharged by the firm's management. What was not in dispute is that, on leaving Lovell, the former employee began working for a competing nursery in the area.

The trial court denied the temporary injunction request. It did not rule on whether the information in dispute was, in fact, a trade secret. Lovell claimed that the specialized growing knowledge acquired by Levy during his employ was a trade secret for which adequate steps had been taken to assure and maintain secrecy. Levy countered that the information in question, which dealt with methods of growing flowers, was not secret and, therefore, was not a trade secret as defined by the UTSA. The UTSA was adopted and became effective in Florida in 1988 and, therefore, was the major statute of concern. The former employee claimed that information on improving one's flower production was well known in the industry and, therefore, was not secret.

An interesting aspect of this case, and one that added to its relatively unique nature, was the fact that the plaintiff firm apparently did not disclose to the court the specific nature of the secrets it claimed had been misappropriated. It must be noted that, in cases alleging misappropriation of trade secrets, one must establish that trade secrets existed and were being utilized or otherwise disclosed in an unauthorized or unapproved manner in order for a remedy to ensue.

Trade secrets under the provisions of the UTSA comprise information that is secret, possesses independent economic value, and for which reasonable steps have been taken to maintain their secrecy. For a court to determine whether or not a trade secret exists, a court must be in a position of being able to delve into the matter by being made privy to the information in dispute. In the absence of any disclosure to the court as to the specific information involved and steps taken to insure secrecy, it is difficult, if not impossible, for a clear determination to be made concerning the protectable nature of the information as a trade secret. Claims of trade secret misappropriation must result in a disclosure to the court of the secret before a determination can be made as to the existence of a legally protectable trade secret. The fact that a court can and will issue protective orders surrounding a secret on request should allow a firm that alleges trade secrets misappropriation some degree of security when pursuing property rights under the law. The trial court's refusal to grant an injunction and its denial to place protective orders on the information claimed to be a trade secret will surprise few given the dearth of information concerning the firm's alleged secrets in the *Lovell* case.

However, at the heart of *Lovell* was the noncompete agreement that the employee purportedly had signed. Irreparable injury to a firm can be presumed if it can show that a valid covenant not to compete has been violated. However, therein is what some may call the catch. The validity of any noncompete agreement must be established and its violation must be shown in order to prove harm. If the noncompete covenant is shown to be invalid, then it or its invalid provisions cannot be enforced. In Florida, where *Lovell* was prosecuted, a statute was enacted and in place that essentially restricts the granting of injunctive relief in cases alleging breaches of noncompete agreements. The statute specifically states that employees may enter into agreements with employers in which they agree to refrain from carrying on or engaging in a similar business "within a reasonably limited time and area." The courts, when deciding whether or not a particular noncompete covenant should be enforced, can take into account the effect that enforcement may have on the public safety, health, or welfare. If enforcement would pose a threat of injury to one of the three public concerns stipulated, a court "shall not" entertain such an order. In addition, Florida law stipulates that courts shall not issue injunctions to enforce "unreasonable" covenants not to compete nor will they enforce covenants not shown to result in irreparable injury. A provision in Florida law that is relevant here, and perhaps commendable, is the stipulation that the misappropriation (use) of a trade secret results in a presumption of irreparable injury and may be specifically enjoined, but the existence of a trade secret and its misuse must be demonstrated for the presumption of irreparable injury and for an injunction to ensue.

The nonfinal order of the circuit court rejected the request for an injunction preventing the former employee from using the alleged trade secrets while working for the competitor. Lovell appealed the decision. The district court of appeal affirmed the order denying the injunction. The court noted that the employer was required to plead and prove the existence and use of a trade secret before a temporary injunction could be issued.

Executives working to develop effective noncompete covenants need to work closely with competent legal counsel to assure the validity of their contracts. Most states have expectations or stipulations surrounding noncompete covenants that are similar to Florida's statute. In short, it is the intent of much federal legislation and many state statutes concerning commerce to encourage competition. Noncompete covenants taken at face value stand in contradiction to legislative and judicial efforts that desire or result in an improved competitive environment. The importance of making sure that noncompete covenants meet expectations of state law cannot be overstated. Other cases, as will be seen, have hinged on whether specific covenants were enforceable. Still, the use of valid noncompete covenants in a work environment adds to the climate of confidentiality that many desire.

In *IMI-Tech Corporation v. Gagliani et al.*, two former employees of a division of International Harvester who had signed personal service agreements forbidding the use or disclosure of trade secrets in future employment were sued to stop their use of secrets that IMI-Tech claimed it owned. As a result of the action, the defendants were enjoined from licensing or making further use of the secrets the plaintiff acquired when it purchased the assets of the International Harvester division.

In *IMI-Tech*, the defendants purportedly were using a process to make fire resistant foam for a firm they established after leaving the employ of International Harvester. The process in question purportedly made use of technology the two had developed in the scope of their International Harvester employment, an action that, if true, might be viewed as violating their personal services agreements. The defendants countered with several arguments, including the fact that their process used a different surfactant in the chemical process than that used by the IMI-Tech process. They also claimed that the process information was not really secret, because much of it could be obtained on request by government agencies (primarily NASA and the Department of Energy) for whom contracts using the process had been fulfilled by IMI-Tech.

IMI-Tech argued successfully for a preliminary injunction by emphasizing that the surfactant used by Gagliani and the new firm was, in fact, very similar in property to their surfactant — so similar, in fact, as to infringe on their trade secrets. In addition, IMI-Tech noted that it had taken several steps that, as a group, provided a climate of confidentiality that, in turn, provided for the protection of their firm's trade secrets. Among these steps was the requirement that employees sign confidentiality agreements that forbade unauthorized disclosure of the firm's trade secrets. In addition, the firm utilized a complicated double-blind purchasing system, which Gagliani himself had made use of while at IMI-Tech. The double-blind purchasing system prevented the disclosure of the surfactant's identity to other employees of the firm. IMI-Tech also reported that it had taken extensive additional security precautions that were deemed necessary to adequately maintain secrecy of its processes when the firm moved its operations from California to Chicago. IMI-Tech considered even the name of the surfactant supplier a trade secret of the firm, because the name of the source of the surfactant was not readily ascertainable by others.

As to the argument that Gagliani proffered that the information was not secret because government agencies could request the information, the plaintiff showed that more than one year had expired since delivery of the contracted materials to the agencies involved. The government contracts involved in this argument stipulated that the purchasing agencies could request IMI-Tech to supply additional information on the materials purchased for up to one year following delivery of the materials. Because the one year time period had expired and no request had been forthcoming, even the purchasing agencies were no longer in a position to delve further into the process or its components. As a result, the confidentiality of the materials and process that IMI-Tech claimed as its trade secrets had not been compromised.

Another item of interest relative to this case is that, in adopting the UTSA, the California legislature removed the phrase "and not being readily ascertainable by proper means by other persons" from its definition of trade secrets as embodied in its version of the UTSA. As a result, in California, it is not a requirement of the state's version of the law that a trade secret not be readily ascertainable by others but, rather, that it had not been ascertained by others at the time of the alleged misappropriation. A violation of express or implied duties of nondisclosure is an example of improper means under the UTSA. Further, it is important to recognize that California law, like the law of many states, has at its core the concept that wrongful acquisition of information should be punished, even if the information in question could have been obtained legally.

The departure of employees and the purported use of proprietary information acquired during the course of employment by former employees in new business ventures have resulted in many cases alleging the misappropriation of trade secrets. As sometimes can be found, the unauthorized use by individuals of allegedly proprietary information in new business pursuits has ended with a decision by a court to enjoin the use or continued disclosure of the information when that information has been deemed to be a trade secret and its use acquired in an unauthorized manner. Trade secrets law in general and the UTSA in particular exist to encourage innovation in business and commerce through the offering of legal protection of proprietary property rights that are not extended through patent or copyright laws.

Various state and federal statutes emphasize that restraints of trade should be avoided and, in many instances, are expressly forbidden. Laws in Montana highlight that state's relatively strict stance that commerce should be encouraged and not restrained. Specifically, Montana law forbids unreasonable agreements that prohibit persons from exercising any lawful trade. Among the issues decided in the case of *State Medical Oxygen and Supply, Inc., v. American Medical Oxygen Company et al.*, was the reasonableness of an employment agreement concerning the expectation that employees not divulge or otherwise misuse State Medical's trade secrets.

American Medical Oxygen Company hired former employees of State Medical Oxygen and Supply, which was one of its competitors. Both firms were involved in the distribution of health care products, including medically approved oxygen, to homebound patients. In addition, they sold oxygen to hospitals and other health care providers. American Medical requires its employees to sign an agreement stipulating that employees will not disclose, either directly or indirectly, its trade secrets and customer lists. State Medical did experience a loss of some customers who changed their accounts to American as a result of its former employees leaving and proceeding to work for the competitor. State Medical filed suit against American and its former employees, alleging, among other factors, a breach of the employment contract by the former employees and misuse of trade secrets.

The Montana trial court found for the former employees and American. State Medical appealed the district court's judgment. The state's supreme court ruled that the employee agreement was not reasonable and was unenforceable in that it violated state law that voided contracts that restrained anyone from conducting lawful business pursuits within the state. It should be noted that a clause in the agreement specified that the agreement was to be considered in effect during the term of the individual's employment with State Medical and "for all time thereafter." That clause and the absence of a reasonable geographic limit in the employment agreement played important roles in the finding that the agreement was unreasonable and that it allowed for the restraint of a lawful profession and, therefore, was unenforceable.

A situation in which a marketing representative for an independent medical examination firm quit and opened her own firm in a city in which she had conducted preliminary marketing research for her former employer resulted in a suit seeking to enjoin her from competing with her former employer. In *Western Medical Consultants, Inc. v. Johnson*, the former employee had agreed to a noncompete covenant in an employment agreement. The employment agreement specifically forbade employees from using the firm's techniques, know-how, ideas, or processes in competing with the firm. The covenant stipulated that the term of the agreement was for five years from the date of a termination of employment and applied to an area within 50 miles of any office operated by the employer. It further stipulated that, after termination, employees agreed not to solicit other employees for the purpose of working in a competing enterprise. Western Medical Consultants, Inc., was a corporation based in Oregon, and the suit that ensued involved that state's UTSA, which became effective in 1987.

A preliminary marketing research study concerning the potential for Western to enter the Alaska market, conducted by Johnson for Western, and actions by Johnson after the initial study was completed and submitted to her employer constituted the basis of the suit by Western. It was reported that Johnson conducted a conscientious study and supplied Western with a report indicating that the Anchorage market held promise for Western's operations. After receiving her report, Western took no immediate action other than to deny Johnson's request for a return trip with the purpose of making a presentation to a group of insurance adjusters and initiating other marketing activities on the behalf of Western. Despite the firm's denial of a second trip or, perhaps, in response to the denial, Johnson purchased a ticket on her own with the purpose of returning to Anchorage and conducting an investigation into the potential for her to open a similar business there. Eventually, Western relented and allowed for the trip. Johnson was unable to make the presentation she had planned before the group of adjusters because of the trip's late authorization, but she did manage to distribute Western's brochures and other information to those in attendance at the adjusters' meeting. Before returning to Oregon, Johnson investigated a potential office location for Western.

Shortly after returning to the office, Johnson resigned her position as marketing representative. She agreed to meet a few days later with her replacement and discuss her findings and efforts on behalf of Western. Because of conflicts on the part of her replacement, such a meeting never took place. However, Johnson informed the management that, should her replacement need any clarification or further information, she should feel free to call Johnson at home.

Shortly thereafter, Johnson left for Anchorage and started an independent medical examination business. Before leaving, she hired her sister who was at the time working for Western as a receptionist. Within the month, Western opened an office in Anchorage. Western then filed suit against Johnson and her firm, seeking to enjoin them from conducting a competing operation. Among Western's charges was the claim that Johnson had violated the employment agreement's covenant not to compete, had hired her sister in violation of the agreement, and had misappropriated its trade secrets. Among its claimed trade secrets were its processes, including its forms, and a list of potential customers developed by Johnson during her first trip to Anchorage.

The U.S. District Court noted that the five year limitation and the restriction as to operating a competing firm within 50 miles of a Western office appeared reasonable under Oregon law and, therefore, was enforceable. However, Johnson's actions were not found to be in violation of the noncompete covenant. When Johnson opened her Anchorage office, Western had no office in the state of Alaska. It could be argued that the firm was considering locating an office there, but the agreement was specific as to the 50 mile radius of an office of Western. Therefore, Johnson's act of locating her office in Anchorage prior to Western's expansion did not violate her express agreement not to compete with Western. As to hiring her sister, testimony revealed that the sister was also her roommate. An offer for her to move with her sister to Alaska was not found to be unreasonable or infringing on the competitive ability of Western. In addition, the court noted that Western had not shown that a receptionist had unique or special value to the firm, and, therefore, the court did not find fault with Johnson's asking her sister to live and work with her in Alaska.

The question raised as to a misappropriation of trade secrets surrounding the potential customer list developed by Johnson was found in favor of the defendant. The court noted that the names of potential customers came from the Anchorage phone book and from other public sources. In short, the names were not secret and were readily ascertainable. Therefore, a misappropriation of trade secrets did not occur. Finally, the court noted that Johnson had conscientiously provided Western "with all of the information she possessed" relative to the Anchorage market, that her efforts in Anchorage as a Western employee were solely on behalf of Western, and that she had not solicited business for her own firm until after she had left the employ of Western. As a result, she had not violated any fiduciary duty owed to Western.

A division of an international food and candy company sued a former sales representative who left the firm's employment to work for a competitor. *Nestle Food Company v. Miller*, filed in Rhode Island, was a case in which an alleged breach of an expressed covenant not to compete became the basis for the food company's effort to seek injunctive relief and damages. Under the state's law, covenants restricting the right of employees to pursue other business ventures are not encouraged and, therefore, are carefully scrutinized as to their reasonableness. Lacking reasonableness, a covenant with an employee restricting competition will not be enforceable.

The division of Nestle for which Miller worked sold candies to schools, associations, charities, community organizations, and other groups interested in reselling the candies to raise funds for their activities. Testimony indicated that the potential customer base for such products was a dynamic market. There was competition for such accounts. The contact names and allied information at potential customer organizations changed regularly, requiring periodic updates. Because of the competition in the market and the regular turnover of contacts, customer loyalty as evidenced by customer retention appeared not to be overwhelming, with repeat orders from one year to the next fluctuating in the neighborhood of 50 to 60 percent.

Miller had been a sales representative for Nestle for approximately 11 years. During what may be described as a successful tenure at Nestle, Miller was responsible for a sales increase of over 1,000 percent. On January 1, 1992, Miller entered into an employment agreement restricting his ability to work for a direct competitor in the same market area during the term of the contract or for a period of one year from a termination of his employment. The contract period was for one year. During the summer of that same year, Miller resigned his position at Nestle and went to work for a competitor.

Nestle filed suit seeking injunctive relief and damages, alleging a breach of the noncompetition covenant. Noting that repeat sales in the territory during the year following Miller's departure dropped almost 20 percent, amounting to approximately $230,000, the firm sought damages and claimed that Miller had misused its customer account information, specifically, the names and contact information of Nestle's potential customers and their purchase histories.

Before reaching a decision, the court first had to determine whether or not the noncompetition covenant was enforceable. The court noted that the time limit specified in the agreement, one year after termination of employment, appeared to be reasonable given the circumstances. However, perhaps surprisingly to some, the court criticized the stipulation that employees could not compete in the same market area in which they formerly had been employed. The court noted that such a stipulation would appear to place an undue burden on employees who would have to move to another geographic location in order to seek work. The court suggested an alternative for potential future use which would have had the effect of preventing unfair competition but without placing the hardship of moving on an individual, that is, it was suggested that such agreements would be better if they restricted employees from soliciting former customers in the trade area and using the confidential information acquired at their place of work for the benefit of a competitor. Still, the court noted that, even given the lesser imposing restrictions as described, Miller's actions would have been construed to have been at odds with the agreement.

The court ruled that Nestle had a right to prohibit the use of its confidential information for the benefit of a competitor and had the right to protect its goodwill. Miller was enjoined from soliciting any customer who had been a customer of Nestle during the year prior to his resignation. He also was enjoined permanently from using information acquired during his tenure with Nestle that was obtained solely as a result of his position with Nestle and that was not readily accessible to others. In the consideration of damages, testimony revealed that 25 former Nestle customers had switched to Miller's new employer. Of those who switched away from Nestle, Miller had solicited approximately 12. The court noted that, based on the testimony, over 100 of Miller's Nestle customers normally would switch to a competitor, given the statistical history of nonrepeat customers. That being the case, the court found that Nestle's computation of damages was entirely speculative. For damages, the court awarded Nestle the sum of $1.

Taquino v. Teledyne Monarch Rubber et al., was a multidimensional case involving a myriad of allegations pertaining to breaches of contract, patent infringements, misappropriations of trade secrets, unfair trade practices, false advertising, and a litany of other charges. In fact, the case, as was finally heard by the U.S. Court of Appeal, was the result of three individual civil suits involving individuals and firms headquartered in three separate states, which had been consolidated for the purposes of the current adjudication. Although the litany of allegations as charged in the consolidated suit are of interest in a general business setting, it is the charge of a misappropriation of trade secrets that is of most interest in the current discussion. Additionally, the impact of an alleged breach of contract involving an agreement not to compete is of interest to those planning strategic efforts to protect trade secrets.

Taquino had been an independent contractor selling industrial products of Teledyne Monarch Rubber to firms situated throughout the region of the Gulf of Mexico. The product line consisted of a variety of rubber items used extensively in the offshore drilling industry. Pursuant to the provisions of the contract Taquino had with Teledyne, Taquino was to receive commissions from Teledyne for his sales of its products but was not considered an employee of Teledyne. According to the information available, employees of Teledyne were expected to sign an "invention agreement" mandating confidentiality surrounding Teledyne's operations and secrets that served as an acknowledgement that the firm's employees recognized that inventions developed at Teledyne were considered to be the property of the firm. Taquino did not sign the invention agreement because he was not an employee. Taquino's relationship with the firm was perceived as that of a self-employed, independent contractor. However, in the contract Taquino signed with Teledyne, there was a noncompetition clause, which served as the basis for one of the charges filed by Teledyne.

This noncompetition clause allowed that, if Teledyne were to terminate the agreed-upon sales relationship, Taquino would be free to compete in the industry without restriction. However, it also stipulated that, should Taquino terminate the agreement, he would refrain from competing in the industry for a period of two years. After working under contract to Teledyne for some time, Teledyne assigned his contract to another firm, an option under one of the contract's provisions. Taquino continued to work for a short period of time. While so engaged, he is alleged to have approached a variety of rubber companies and component parts companies and begun looking for a manufacturer that could produce a product purportedly of his design. It appears that, at that time, he began efforts to seek patent protection for his product and even conducted a market survey as an apparent prelude to entering the market on his own. Shortly thereafter, he resigned and started his own firm. The three cases that were consolidated ensued, with charges and cross-charges being brought to bear.

One of the questions to be decided was whether or not the express noncompetition clause was a valid and enforceable contract. At first consideration, the answer appears to be easy, but as in many points of contention that are investigated closely under a legal magnifying glass, things are not what they always seem; that is why it is very important to have one's legal counsel develop a noncompetition clause that would withstand scrutiny. Two points of concern for noncompetition clauses were recognized in the court's deliberations. First, the clause prohibited Taquino from competing for a period of two years. The two year period was seen as reasonable by the courts and, thus, enforceable. Second, it seems that this provision of the contract did not include any territorial limits to the competition. As was pointed out, a restrictive covenant that contains no territorial limitations is unreasonable and, therefore, cannot be enforced.

Courts look closely at noncompetition clauses in contracts because noncompetition clauses in and of themselves can be construed as anticompetitive. Congress and state legislatures have passed numerous acts with the purpose of encouraging or maintaining competition in the marketplace. As a result, courts look closely at contracts that discourage competition and expect that the limitations imposed by such agreements be reasonable. In other words, an agreement that limited a party to the contract to "never" again enter the industry would be deemed to be anticompetitive and unreasonable. Likewise, the courts expect territorial limitations as to the extent of the agreement. Had Taquino's contract clause limited his competition for two years to the region of the Gulf of Mexico, that might have garnered the full support of the court.

In this case, the charge that Taquino had misappropriated trade secrets revolved around a particular piece of equipment and knowledge of upcoming jobs being let out for bid. The court noted that there was no evidence presented to indicate that the piece of equipment in question was kept confidential from parties outside the employment of Teledyne Monarch Rubber. Indeed, it was revealed that another firm's employees had been involved in its testing. Additionally, the information that Taquino possessed about potential contracts to be let out for bid was not shown to be anything other than what all firms competing in the market had access to as a regular part of their being in the business.

For those interested, despite the unenforceable provision in the noncompetition clause and despite not having a charge of misappropriation against him upheld, Taquino was, nevertheless, faulted for breach of another provision of his contract that forbade his representing a competing company prior to the termination of the contract with Teledyne. His efforts to establish his own firm and market it while under contract to

Teledyne were found to be in violation of the express provisions of the agreement.

There have been other cases revolving around trade secrets disputes and the enforceability of employment agreements that aim to curtail competition by former employees who possess specific knowledge of a former employer's trade secrets. A case in point is *Ackerman v. Kimball International, Inc.* This action represented the appeal of the former employee (Ackerman) to the trial court's decision to enforce a covenant not to compete while enjoining Ackerman from making use of information deemed to be a trade secret belonging to Kimball International (the former employer). The information in question, which the court determined to be a proprietary trade secret, involved a listing of customers and suppliers and specific pricing information.

It appears from the record that Ackerman's employment with Kimball was terminated pursuant to a provision in an employment agreement to which Ackerman was party, reserving such a right to the firm. As per the agreement, Ackerman purportedly received a severance package comprising compensation in the form of specified severance pay and various benefits. Further, it was reported that Ackerman immediately accepted employment with a competing firm. Kimball quickly sought a temporary restraining order and a preliminary injunction to prevent its former employee from pursuing such a competitive position, charging that it violated provisions of the employment agreement to which he was bound. Among the agreement's provisions was a covenant not to compete. The charges were brought to bear under the terms of the employment agreement and under the auspices of the state's (Indiana's) UTSA. Indiana adopted the UTSA in 1982, approximately 11 years prior to the filing of this case.

Ackerman's case revolved around several issues. Among the more relevant issues to this discussion were two that concerned whether the customer list and pricing information could be construed to be a trade secret and whether the employment agreement was enforceable. As can be surmised, if a trade secret is shown not to exist, then there can be no misappropriation (or threatened misappropriation), and an injunction regarding such information restraint would not ensue. In addition, if the employment agreement was unenforceable, Ackerman would be free to work for the competing firm.

Background information from the case indicates that Ackerman had worked for Kimball for approximately 11 years prior to being asked to sign the employment agreement, which stipulated that Kimball would continue to employ Ackerman and, for his part, Ackerman agreed not to compete with Kimball for one year following a termination. The agreement also required Ackerman to safeguard certain confidential business information belonging to Kimball. Ackerman had been elevated to the position of executive vice president within a division of Kimball, which gave him direct responsibility for four of Kimball's operating plants. However, it was reported that Ackerman later was demoted to the position of general manager. It appeared that the demotion occurred slightly more than one year prior to the filing of the charges in this action. Shortly thereafter, Ackerman received and declined an offer of employment from a competing firm. Later, the competitor reportedly sweetened its offer by offering Ackerman a position as vice president of its U.S. operations at a salary in excess of his highest salary at Kimball. Around the middle of his last month in the employ of Kimball, Ackerman supposedly asked for and received lists compiled from the firm's data base that included the names of both the suppliers and the customers of one of Kimball's divisions.

The very next day, Ackerman was informed that he was being terminated. He was presented with a termination agreement that stipulated that he would be given $15,000 in severance pay and additional benefits, including placement counseling. In exchange for the severance package, Ackerman had to agree not to use Kimball's trade secrets in future employment. A stipulation in the agreement specified that it did not supersede the provisions of the employment agreement signed by Ackerman more than a decade previously. A copy of that agreement also was given to the terminated employee. The termination agreement was agreed to by Ackerman, and shortly thereafter, he received the severance pay as called for in the agreement. Almost immediately after leaving the employ of Kimball, Ackerman accepted the offer of employment by the competitor. The suit by Kimball seeking to enjoin the former employee from working for the competitor and from using its trade secrets quickly ensued.

In deliberating on the enforceability of the original employment agreement, the court found, contrary to Ackerman's claims, that consideration did exist in the form of the promise of future employment at the time the contract was signed. The fact that the agreement contained a provision that allowed Kimball to terminate the employment at will did not diminish the fact that there was an offer of continued employment in the agreement, an offer that places an obligation on the employer. The offer of continued employment was seen as sufficient consideration to enforce the contract. As has been seen in other cases, the adequacy of consideration is not an issue for a court to decide but is, instead, an issue for contracting parties to decide. The fact that consideration existed in the form of a promise of continued at-will employment did constitute sufficient consideration on the part of Kimball. Coupled with the consideration on the part of Ackerman, the agreement was seen as containing valid consideration on the part of both parties, making the agreement enforceable as to the existence of consideration. Perhaps not important to the deliberation but of potential interest to many is the recognition in the record that Ackerman was employed by Kimball for almost 20 years after the execution of the original employment agreement.

Pursuant to its charges under the auspices of the state's trade secrets law, Kimball prevailed in its claim that the customer and supplier information constituted protectable trade secrets. It appeared that reasonable measures to secure the information, given the circumstances, were in effect and maintained by the firm in a manner to assure the continued secrecy of the information. The information was shown not to be generally available or known in the industry. The information was shown to possess independent economic value as required of protectable trade secrets. The court found that the information in dispute met the elements necessary to indicate the existence of a protectable trade secret.

The trial court's finding that Kimball was entitled to a preliminary injunction that would enjoin Ackerman's threatened disclosure, use, or misappropriation of its trade secrets was upheld by the court of appeals. The appeal also resulted in the confirmation that sufficient consideration existed to enforce the terms of the employment agreement. Again, it should be remembered that the UTSA specifies that "threatened misappropriations" may be enjoined. Indeed, in this case, it could be argued that Ackerman would not have had time to make use of the secrets to which he was privy prior to the legal action by Kimball. An important implication for strategic management efforts is that an actual misappropriation does not have to occur in order for an employer to gain an injunction in cases in which former employees pose serious misappropriation threats.

One more thought about covenants not to compete or covenants not to disclose is that the parties to a covenant, especially those in top management positions who are charged with protecting the firm's secrets, should take covenants or agreements with employees or others at face value, that is, the courts are going to use the simple, normal, everyday interpretation of terms and concepts included in such agreements. It is especially important to recognize that, if such agreements are lacking in some manner as to a desired outcome on the part of the employee or other party, the court will not inject some postagreement meaning pursuant to a desire of management or the former employee. In essence, it is not the court's job to rewrite a contract under the auspices of a court decision in order to achieve some equitable result relative to a provision seen as lacking in a valid contract.

A case example involved a pet food distributor and manufacturer that had entered into an agreement pursuant to a distributor relationship established by contract. In *All West Pet Supply Company v. Hill's Pet Products Division, Colgate-Palmolive Company*, the provisions of a contract involving the disposition of trade secrets came into question upon the contract's termination. All West Pet Supply is a pet food distributor that had a distributorship agreement with Hill's Pet Products. Pursuant to the contract, All West furnished customer information to Hill's on a periodic basis for use in a sales management data base system. As a provision in the contract, Hill's Pet Products was obligated to keep the information confidential during the term of the contract. The contract stated that the written agreement embodied the entire agreement of the parties relative to the distributorship arrangement and mutual responsibilities and that any modifications to the agreement must be made in writing and, ostensibly, with the agreement of both parties. The distributorship contract expired, and then questions were raised about the obligation of Hill's to not use or disclose the information All West had supplied and that Hill held in its sales management data base system.

All West sued, charging breach of contract and misappropriation of trade secrets. A central concern of the case was the fact that Hill's Pet Products was expected to keep the information confidential pursuant to the terms of the contract. As the lower court found and as was upheld on appeal, the contract's provision requiring the distributor to provide the customer information to Hill's and Hill's obligation to maintain the confidentiality of the information both ceased to exist on the expiration of the contract. As the court noted, a contract that is specific as to its duration generally terminates upon its expiration. Once the contract expires, the mutual obligations of the parties involved cease to exist unless the parties provide expressly for some other contingency in the contract. Because the contract specifically spelled out that all obligations to the contract were embodied in the agreement and that changes to it must have been in writing, it expired as written.

As was stated in the first order granting a partial summary judgment for the defendant, "it is not the function of the court to rewrite a contract." In such instances, the court is not interested in trying to achieve someone's idea of an equitable result; it is interested only in enforcing contracts pursuant to the law. This case emphasizes the importance of making sure that provisions of agreements aimed at restricting the use of trade secrets clearly delineate the disposition of trade secrets and the obligations of all parties upon contract expiration.

It is important to recognize that maintaining a climate of confidentiality is at the heart of this discussion. Firms that are lax in their confidentiality procedures and policies will find they may come up short when confronted with a misappropriation.

Among other steps that a firm can take to develop a climate of confidentiality is the imposition of physical security surrounding the secrets. Insisting on the secrets being secured in locked file cabinets in restricted areas is an easy-to-implement factor that can add to the desired climate. Access restrictions on visitors and others who have no need to know the secrets could add to the climate. Requiring the destruction of surplus copies of secret information and numerous other precautionary steps can contribute to a climate of confidentiality that will encourage employees to recognize and maintain a firm's trade secrets. Charles Plueddeman (1995) describes the extent of security measures Mercury Marine has instituted surrounding the development of new propellors. The firm reportedly conducts tests of new designs in an undisclosed lake location at night, using underwater cameras and strobe lights. Chase boats accompany the test boat to ward off intruders and provide other security measures. Mercury Marine rightly takes the concept of maintaining trade secrets security seriously and has developed a climate of confidentiality aimed at protecting its competitive stance.

The need for the creation of a climate of confidentiality cannot be overemphasized. The theft of proprietary information and its negative impact on a variety of firms appears to be on the rise. According to Lawrence Ingrassia (1990), General Electric reported it had suffered nine significant leaks of its trade secrets in one five-year period. A report by P. Doe (1988) indicated that two-thirds of Japanese firms surveyed believed they had been damaged by the violation of their intellectual property rights, including the misappropriation of their trade secrets. Michael Miller (1992) reported that IBM filed suit against a former employee who had not disclosed trade secrets but whom IBM perceived as posing "an egregious threat" to the security of its trade secrets. Such an apparently unprecedented legal action by IBM, which, at the time, was accompanied by "warnings" to ten other former IBM employees, is indicative of the value that certain firms place on trade secrets and on the perceived damage that may occur from their misappropriation. Wendy Zellner and Bruce Hager (1991) discuss how Mary Kay Cosmetics discovered that its trash had been the target of agents of another international cosmetics firm. The competitor cosmetics firm's agents were intent on discovering "secrets" that had been thrown away, and when the agents were discovered, they were in possession of company documents containing potentially sensitive information. A story by Anne Reifenberg (1995) details how the owners of "Slick 50" recently were the target of an extortionist; someone with a copy of its secret formula, a formula for which substantial security had been provided, was offering the formula for ransom. Luckily for the firm's owners, an individual was arrested in the case and a copy of the formula reportedly recovered.

In perhaps what is a sign of the times, a report in *Datamation* (1993) observed that an advisor to the U.S. Department of State on security affairs reported that U.S. business firms are increasingly the target of foreign spies intent on stealing U.S. business secrets. A report by Glenn R. Simpson (1995) detailed how a software company might have committed industrial espionage with the help of, or under the guise of, needing software for an unnamed, secret federal agency. Business executives are being warned not to disclose secrets to "students" conducting school projects for fear that such students actually may be corporate spies or agents of foreign governments. The direct cost of trade secrets misappropriation is in the billions of dollars annually. A firm desiring to protect its trade secrets should begin by developing and fostering a climate of confidentiality in which the value of its trade secrets is recognized and plans are in place to protect them.

SUMMARY OF CONCEPTS

1. A climate of confidentiality should be established in one's workplace.

2. A legal nondisclosure covenant may add to the climate desired and improve the chance that secrets will be maintained.

3. A legal noncompetition covenant may add to the climate desired and improve the chances that secrets will not be utilized against the original owner.

4. Employment agreements must be legal as to time and place in order to be enforceable.

5. The reasonableness of stipulations included in restrictive covenants or employment contracts plays a major factor in determining the legality of the stipulations.

6. State laws vary as to definitions or expectations of reasonableness as it relates to employment contracts.

7. Competent legal counsel should be sought in the early stages of strategic planning related to the protection of trade secrets.

8. The cost of trade secrets misappropriation is in the billions of dollars annually.

9. Executives need to be careful not to disclose trade secrets to individuals without a need to know.

EXAMPLES OF COVENANTS NOT TO COMPETE

These example covenants are for informational purposes, provided only for discussion, and should not be construed to be legal advice or necessarily valid in a specific jurisdiction. Get legal assistance when preparing such covenants. (Contributed by John W. Yeargain.)

Example Covenant 1

Any person, including a corporation and the individual shareholders of such corporation, who is employed as an agent, servant, or employee, shall agree to refrain from carrying on or engaging in a business similar to that of the employer and/or from soliciting customers of the employer within any and all designated areas in which the employer is currently operating or plans to be operating within the next (number that is reasonable according to state) years.

Example Covenant 2

For (number — check state statute for maximum) years after termination of employee's employment for any reason, employee shall not, within a (county or municipality or [number]-mile radius) of employer's present places of business, own, manage, operate, or control any business similar to that conducted by employer. Nor for (number) years after termination of employment for any reason shall employee usurp any business opportunity for expansion into new areas from employer of which employee was aware of or should have been aware of prior to termination.

EXAMPLE OF NONDISCLOSURE/ NONCOMPETE CONTRACT

These example covenants are for informational purposes, provided only for discussion, and should not be construed to be legal advice or necessarily valid in a specific jurisdiction. Get legal assistance when preparing such covenants. (Contributed by Renée D. Culverhouse.)

Definition of Confidential Information

As used in this employment contract, "confidential information" refers to any and all information disclosed to the undersigned employee or which may become known to the undersigned employee because of or due to his or her relationship or status as such employee concerning the employer's products, merchandise, output, processes, procedures, operations, and services which are not generally known in the business, industry, or field engaged in by the employer at the time of or subsequent to the execution of this agreement. This includes information relating to accounting, billing, customer lists, engineering, research and development, manufacture, pricing, purchasing, marketing, merchandising, and sales and distribution. This information may or may not have been labeled by the employer as confidential information.

Prohibition against Disclosure

Undersigned employee acknowledges that the information referred to above is confidential and that it is a valuable and unique asset of the business of the employer. As such, the information will remain at all times the property of the employer, regardless of its physical location or dissemination. Undersigned employee hereby expressly promises and agrees never to use, reveal, publish, disseminate, disclose, or distribute in any manner any such confidential information, either by direct or indirect means or methods, without obtaining the prior written consent of employer. This restriction applies not only during the term of employment but after the end of such relationship as well. Further, upon the termination of the employment relationship, the undersigned employee expressly agrees that all documents, records, notebooks, files, electronic data, computer diskettes and/or tapes and any and all copies or reproductions or facsimiles thereof, whether the product of the undersigned employee or others, will remain in the possession of the employer.

Remedies for Breach of This Agreement

Upon receiving notice of the breach, intent to breach, or threat to breach the provisions of this agreement by the undersigned employee, employer may seek relief in the form of temporary or permanent injunctions or restraining orders, prohibiting the undersigned employee from disclosing any and all confidential information. Such injunctions or restraining orders shall further prohibit the undersigned employee from using such confidential information in the service of any individual, person, firm, partnership, corporation, association, or other organization. Employer may also seek other relief, including the recovery of damages (actual, compensatory, consequential, punitive, and/or otherwise) available for breach (actual, anticipatory, or threatened) of this agreement.

Terms or Conditions of Employment

The above paragraphs relating to the disclosure of confidential information and/or trade secrets of the employer are hereby acknowledged and considered by both parties to be terms or conditions of employment of the undersigned employee.

Governing Law

This agreement shall be construed according to and in strict compliance with and shall be governed by the laws of the State of _____.

APPENDIX: CITATIONS AND MANAGEMENT IMPLICATIONS

ITT Telecom Products Corporation v. Dooley 262 Cal.Rptr. 773 (Cal.App. 6 Dist. 1989) — A climate of confidentiality should be developed. Confidentiality agreements should play a role in the employment process.

Machen, Inc. v. Aircraft Design, Inc. et al. 828 P.2d 73 (Wash.App. 1992) — Discussing a trade secret in a public forum can result in the secret being lost.

Lovell Farms, Inc. v. Levy 641 So.2d 103 (Fla.App. 3 Dist. 1994) — Covenants restricting commerce need to be legal as to time and place. The existence of trade secrets and their misuse must be established in order to claim misappropriation.

IMI-Tech Corporation v. Gagliani et al. 691 F.Supp. 214 (S.D.Cal. 1986) — Confidentiality agreements must play a role in the fostering of an atmosphere of confidentiality. Other steps need to be taken to insure secrecy.

State Medical Oxygen and Supply, Inc., v . American Medical Oxygen Company et al. 782 P.2d 1272 (Mont. 1989) — Covenants not to compete must be reasonable. They must be limited by time and place considerations. Unreasonable covenants not to compete will be unenforceable.

Western Medical Consultants, Inc. v. Johnson 835 F.Supp. 554 (D.Or. 1993) — Covenants not to compete differ as to their reasonableness. Specific wording of the covenant is important to prevent misunderstandings that may lead to court proceedings.

Nestle Food Company v. Miller 836 F.Supp. 69 (D.R.I. 1993) — Noncompete covenants must be reasonable. Statements that preclude an employee from soliciting former customers after termination and that prohibit the use of confidential information may be enforced.

Taquino v. Teledyne Monarch Rubber et al. 893 F.2d 1488 (5th Cir. 1990) — Covenants not to compete must be legal as to time and place. Secrecy must be maintained to qualify information as a trade secret.

Ackerman v. Kimball International, Inc. 634 N.E.2d 778 (Ind.App. 1 Dist. 1994) — Reasonable covenants not to compete will be enforced. Customer lists can be trade secrets if not readily ascertainable by proper means and if reasonable security has been provided to maintain secrecy.

All West Pet Supply Company v. Hill's Pet Products Division, Colgate-Palmolive Company 847 F.Supp. 858 (D.Kan. 1994) — Agreements not to compete or not to disclose need to be complete and specific as to the disposition of shared secrets and the obligations of parties involved. Courts will not fix your mistakes.

4

Specifying Information to be Protected

Information for which a firm desires Uniform Trade Secrets Act (UTSA) protection must be delineated and specific as to its scope. The courts have been consistent in their interpretations of the UTSA that any information or trade secret for which UTSA protection is sought must be specifically defined. This puts the onus on the members of management during their strategic efforts to protect their firm's property rights to adequately delineate which information the firm considers a secret.

Not all information that an employee learns of or has access to during the course of employment will qualify as a trade secret. In fact, the majority of information with which one's employees are likely to deal in their work could not be described as any kind of secret. In an accounting department, for instance, the use of double entry bookkeeping is a widespread, standard practice in most industries. For an accounting executive to claim that a firm's use of double entry bookkeeping constitutes a trade secret and that the firm deserves court protection for the practice would be ludicrous, and the attempt, understandably, would fail in court.

Newton (1939) relates a non–trade secrets situation that occurred over 100 years ago, when a relatively young attorney posed a question as to how many legs a sheep would have if one were to consider the sheep's tail a leg. Abraham Lincoln, the attorney and new president, posing the question, amused many by answering his own question with the response that the sheep still would have four legs. He explained that, just because someone may call a tail a leg, it doesn't make it a leg. The analogy holds for some proprietary information. Just because some business executives may proffer that they are in possession of information that they consider a trade secret does not necessarily make the information a trade secret under trade secrets law.

For example, take a situation in which a firm's customer account information is considered a trade secret by the owner and executive of a firm. Will or does a court recognize that a customer list is a trade secret deserving protection under trade secrets law? The answer is both yes and no. Specific circumstances surrounding a particular firm's customer list will provide the answer as to whether customer account information is considered a trade secret eligible for legal protection. The circumstances that will determine the legal standing of the information are imbedded in the actions a firm pursues relative to delineating and protecting its customer list under the provisions of its state's trade secrets law.

In the past, firms seeking protection of customer lists as trade secrets have both enjoyed successes and suffered failures in attempts to gain legal protection of customer lists as trade secrets. The difference between those firms that have been successful and those that have failed usually can be traced to actions that meet or fail to meet expectations as detailed in the UTSA. Specific cases and examples of their impact on understanding the scope of the UTSA will be presented in a later chapter. However, it cannot be emphasized enough that individuals desiring protection of proprietary information considered a trade secret need to understand the UTSA and pursue protective efforts that would be reasonable under the circumstances to provide for continued secrecy.

To garner legal protection for one's trade secrets, one must show that reasonable steps were taken to assure their secrecy. In order to do this, one must be able to delineate which information a firm possesses that it considers a trade secret and relate reasonable efforts to that specific information. Firms that fail to delineate which specific information they possess that they consider to be a trade secret open themselves to criticism and, potentially, a loss of their secrets.

A case in point, *Electro-Craft Corporation v. Controlled Motion, Incorporated et al.*, revealed, to the dismay of some, that the mere signing of a nondisclosure agreement does not always provide the legal protection and remedy sought under the UTSA. In this case, the Minnesota Supreme Court held that Electro-Craft Corporation had not proven the existence of a trade secret because of its failure to make reasonable efforts to maintain the secrecy of its process. Even though the firm required employees to sign an employment agreement that included a confidentiality provision (but not a noncompetition agreement), the court held that the agreement was too vague to apprise the employees as to which specific information the firm considered to be secret. It also was noted that confidentiality procedures were lax, for example, motor diagrams were thrown away rather than destroyed and technical documents were not marked "confidential."

The *Electro-Craft* decision's impact on confidentiality agreements and resulting employee expectations relative to recognizing and maintaining trade secrets protection cannot be overemphasized. If a firm wants to protect its secrets, it must decide which information it possesses that qualifies as a trade secret. Then, it must make employees aware of the firm's delineation of that information as a trade secret belonging to the firm and pursue effective avenues of protection that would be reasonable under the circumstances to protect the secret.

In the absence of a specific delineation of which information a firm considers a trade secret, a court will not be in a position to offer a firm the protection and remedy it may seek under the UTSA. The information for which protection is desired must be specified and its secrecy status understood by employees. If employees are not apprised as to which information a firm considers secret, then there can be no realistic expectation that they will be in a position to recognize their duties of confidentiality surrounding the secret. In short, if an individual does not know a certain piece of information is secret, the courts will take the position that there can be no expectation that the individual will not disclose or use the information, potentially to the owner's disadvantage.

The lesson to be learned here is that written confidentiality agreements and policies regarding trade secrets need to be specific as to which information the firm considers a trade secret. This will enhance a firm's efforts to protect its secrets. Such an effect will go beyond the scope of the courtroom; indeed, it is hoped that it would prevent or minimize the need to ever go near a courtroom.

Specifying the information that the firm considers secret should enable an executive to better target the firm's strategic efforts to protect the secret. By recognizing which specific information the firm owns that is secret, an executive is in a better position to impose effective secrecy efforts, such as assuring that the information is secured behind locked doors, that computer access procedures are developed where appropriate, that policies are in place and enforced that assure the destruction of surplus or unneeded copies, and other potential avenues to maintain secrecy of the information are developed. A firm's management will benefit in its protection efforts if it recognizes which specific information it possesses can be construed to be a trade secret and takes appropriate steps.

In *Gordon Employment, Inc. v. Jewell*, an employment agency and its owner sued a former manager for theft of client lists that they considered to be trade secrets. Reportedly, the former employee started her own employment agency after being fired by Gordon. The court held that the client list was not a trade secret under the UTSA because Gordon had made no effort to keep the list confidential. It was revealed that the list was kept in an unlocked file cabinet in a public reception area and was not labeled as confidential and that Gordon had no written policy regarding the confidentiality of the information or providing for its security.

By failing to specify that Gordon Employment considered its client list a trade secret and that it was not to be disclosed to others or used in future employment, Gordon found itself in a position of not having its client list declared a trade secret. Gordon would have profited from having a confidentiality agreement in place that specifically identified the client list as a trade secret belonging to the firm. In addition, placing the information in unlocked file cabinets situated in public reception areas and failing to mark the client list folders as containing confidential information contributed little, if anything, to establishing and maintaining an atmosphere of confidentiality.

Remember, it is important that an atmosphere of confidentiality must pervade the firm and surround the secret. For such to occur, one must specify which information is secret and take appropriate actions to protect the secret. Without specifying which information is secret, taking reasonable steps to protect a firm's secret would be difficult, if not impossible. Only by specifying trade secret information as secret can a firm expect that its employees will be in a position of knowing which information can or, more importantly, cannot be disclosed to others or utilized in unapproved enterprises.

In *Nationwide Mutual Insurance Company v. Stenger*, the large insurer failed in its attempt to restrain the defendant in a subsequent employment from using customer lists obtained during the defendant's employment by the plaintiff. As background, Connecticut law bars employees from utilizing knowledge acquired during a term of employment for their benefit during that term of employment in such a manner as to injure their employer. As one might surmise, such an expectation arises from the common law's contractual expectations surrounding the responsibilities and duties inherent in principal and agent relationships. Further, after a period of employment, individuals are expected to refrain from using, for their own advantage or their new employer's advantage to the detriment of their former employer, trade secrets acquired during their former employ.

In this case, it was alleged that Stenger began using Nationwide's customer lists prior to the end of his employment agreement with Nationwide, to the firm's disadvantage. The district court noted that, with respect to the claimed breach of contract, Stenger's conscious decision to become an agent for two other companies and to solicit business from Nationwide policyholders during the course of his agreement with Nationwide was a violation of a provision of the employment agreement that prohibited such acts. For such a breach of contract, the court noted that Nationwide may be entitled to an accounting (damages). Again, Connecticut law bars the use of knowledge acquired by an employee or agent during employment to the injury of his or her employer during the term of his or her employment.

More central to this case and to an improved understanding of the UTSA, though, is the question of whether or not the customer lists that were in the possession of Stenger constituted trade secrets and whether or not Stenger's actions after the conclusion of his employment with Nationwide constituted a misappropriation of those secrets. Among its remedies, Nationwide sought to enjoin Stenger from making use of the customer lists, because it claimed the lists were among its trade secrets and that Stenger was in the process of misappropriating them.

In its deliberations concerning the requested injunction, the court focused on the wording of Connecticut law that states that, after a period of hire has ceased, an employee or agent has a duty to the employer or principal not to use trade secrets acquired during the period of hire for the benefit of the employee or agent and to the detriment of the former employer or principal. The court denied the injunction sought by Nationwide in finding that the customer lists in Stenger's possession could not be construed to be trade secrets. It was proffered that Nationwide had not instituted reasonable measures to limit access to files and to prevent their disclosure to others. Indeed, the court found that Nationwide had no policy regarding the nondisclosure of information contained in the physical customer files in the possession of Stenger. Further, Nationwide did not have a nondisclosure policy relating to its centralized computer system containing information on policyholders to which Stenger had access during his term of employment.

In reaching its decision, the court noted that a number of factors have to be considered in assessing whether or not a particular information item can be construed to be a trade secret. Each of these factors is taken into consideration by the court when assessing whether or not a particular item can be construed to be a trade secret.

First, consideration of the extent to which the information is known outside the business must figure in the analysis. Obviously, information cannot be a secret if it is widely known outside the business that claims it as a trade secret. Information that is not secret cannot be considered the proprietary property of someone, worthy of protection by the law. Only if a firm possesses secret information can it potentially be considered a trade secret.

Second, the extent to which the information is known by employees and others involved in the business needs to be considered. A secure secret will, undoubtedly, be one that is available only to those with a need to know the information. Information known by everyone or potentially available to everyone in a firm presents a situation in which secrecy may be doubtful or difficult to prove. Allowing only those individuals with a need to know the information access to it will enhance one's contention that the information is a trade secret.

Third, the extent of measures taken by the owner (employer) to maintain the secrecy of the information needs to be ascertained. The UTSA expects efforts that are reasonable under the circumstances to maintain the secrecy of trade secrets. Securing the information in locked file cabinets in locked rooms may lend credence to the claim that the information's secrecy is maintained and that the information is of significant value to the owner. In the absence of such measures, a court would find it difficult to buy the argument that particular information was a trade secret, deserving of its concern and protection.

Fourth, the court would assess the value of the information to the owner and his or her competitors. The UTSA is aimed at protecting information of value. Significant commercial value to the owner and potential value to a competitor should the competitor acquire the information will be expected by the courts to show relevance under the UTSA. The concept of value and the expectations of courts relative to value will be discussed further in Chapter 5.

The fifth factor considered centers around the amount of money spent by the owner (employer) in developing the information. Such a determination aids in assessing the value of the information. A secret that costs nothing for a firm to acquire will be difficult to be proved a trade secret worthy of court protection. Again, the concept of value will be discussed in Chapter 5.

The sixth factor concerns the ease or difficulty with which the information could be acquired or duplicated properly by competitors. The more difficulty such a process entails, the more likely it is that a firm will obtain the recognition of its secrets as sought through the courts. If the information can be obtained easily or readily through proper channels, a firm will have a difficult time having a court recognize its secrets as trade secrets.

The courts also look at the extent to which the principal-agent relationship was of a confidential or fiduciary nature. This seventh factor points out the importance that courts are placing on expectations that duties imposed by principal-agent relationships are a consequence of the relationship. As seen in *Nationwide*, the courts expect that agents will adhere to their duty not to compromise a principal's or employer's position.

Eighth, the courts look closely at the method by which the former agent acquired the alleged secret. Information that was known by an agent or employee to be a trade secret and that was removed from an employer's possession with the intent of depriving the employer of its proprietary property will probably easily be construed to have been a misappropriated trade secret. On the other hand, widespread dissemination of information that a firm considers to be a trade secret will, undoubtedly, have a negative impact on a firm's attempt to garner protection for the secret.

The ninth area that courts will consider in their deliberations revolves around the former agent's personal relationship with the customers on a contested list. Agreements between principals and agents cannot keep third parties (customers) from pursuing their own agendas. Unilateral account switching on the part of customers who have developed personal relationships with their agents cannot be prevented. However, blatant solicitation in violation of contract law as it relates to the UTSA potentially would find little favor in the court.

Finally, the last factor that courts might consider revolves around the existence of any unfair advantage that might accrue to a former agent from the use of the former employer's trade secret. Courts undoubtedly would look with a jaundiced eye on situations resulting in unfair advantage that accrues from a secrets misappropriation.

Firms desiring to protect adequately their confidential trade secret information should start by discerning which information they possess, if any, could be construed to be a trade secret. Trade secrets comprise secret information of value that give a firm a competitive advantage and for which reasonable steps have been taken to maintain their secrecy. In strategic planning to protect trade secrets, executives need to specify which information needs protection. Once the information needing protection is discerned, steps may be pursued that would allow for the reasonable assurance that the information will remain the proprietary property of the firm.

Firms come into possession of a great deal of information that could never be considered a trade secret. Only valuable information that is secret and for which reasonable steps have been taken to maintain secrecy can qualify as a protectable secret. The information that one collects as one goes through life is, more often than not, general knowledge and could not be construed to be anyone's secrets. To ensure the enforceability of employment contracts that have trade secrets provisions, it is important to include stipulations as to exactly which information the firm possesses and considers to be a trade secret.

Business executives and others easily can recognize the need to provide for the protection of proprietary information that possesses value and that serves as a competitive advantage or benefit to the owner. Many can understand the reasoning behind the establishment of trade secrets law aimed at protecting proprietary information and are in favor of punishing those who would take such information and misuse it. However, the question that raises a concern is what to do about information or knowledge that an employer may consider a trade secret but is obtained in the course of an employee's normal business activities and is construed by the employee as part and parcel of his or her general knowledge base. In other words, are former employees expected to "wipe their memories clean" when they leave one employer and go to work for another?

In the case of *Fleming Sales Company, Inc. v. Bailey*, the question of whether an employee is expected to refrain from using his or her accumulated knowledge of a business or industry and, in effect, is required to forget everything he or she may have learned at a former place of employment and not make use of the accumulated knowledge in future employment opportunities paralleled the discussion as to whether or not trade secrets had been misappropriated. In *Fleming*, the firm brought claims against the former employee that included a misappropriation of its trade secrets. The information claimed to have been misappropriated consisted of names on a customer list, the customer contact information contained on the list, and specific information as to the principals associated with the major firms in the industry.

Bailey had worked for Fleming Sales Company in a variety of positions for approximately seven years. Fleming was a privately owned firm acting as sales representatives for manufacturers involved in producing products intended primarily for the recreational vehicle market. It was reported that Bailey, originally hired as a sales representative, was promoted quickly to general manager of the firm's original equipment manufacturing (OEM) division. As evidence of his value to the firm, just a few years later, Bailey accepted an appointment to the firm's board of directors. Purportedly, the

OEM division did well under Bailey's tutelage, and this undoubtedly served as a catalyst for his relatively quick rise in the firm's management ranks. However, despite his successes at Fleming, it was reported that he was less than satisfied, because of what he perceived as a less-than-optimal level of executive freedom afforded his position and because of perceived career limits arising from his working in a closely owned family business. During his last April working for Fleming, Bailey sent a letter of resignation to the board, detailing his dissatisfaction and announcing his intent to leave the firm on May 1. Despite the May 1 date in his letter, Bailey stayed on until the middle of May and received compensation from Fleming through the entire month. It was reported that, during his employment with Fleming, Bailey had not signed or otherwise agreed to any written employment contract nor had he agreed to a covenant not to compete should he leave the firm.

To complicate matters somewhat, Bailey and a partner began a firm with the purpose of producing window blinds to be sold to the recreational vehicle market. The firm was established a few months prior to Bailey's leaving the employ of Fleming, though, reportedly, it did not begin operations until after Bailey had departed. A month after leaving, Bailey and his partner formed a second firm that competed directly with Fleming's OEM division's efforts. Subsequently, several of Fleming's employees were hired by Bailey's newest firm, and that firm began conducting business with some of Fleming's former customers and principal manufacturers. Approximately two months later, Fleming filed suit under the provisions of Indiana's UTSA, claiming that Bailey and his firm were using trade secrets that had been misappropriated from Fleming. Fleming claimed that the misappropriation grew from the misuse of information Bailey had obtained during the course of his employment at Fleming and that the information was protectable as a trade secret. Among the information at issue were the names and addresses of customers, information about customer purchasing and payment histories, and information about sources of supply and specific contractual information concerning the acquisition of products from those suppliers.

The major focus of the case centered on whether the information in question was a trade secret, as Fleming asserted. If the information does not qualify as a trade secret under the state's UTSA, then Fleming has no recourse against Bailey, because he was under no covenant restricting his competing in the business. On the other hand, if the information qualifies as a trade secret, then Fleming potentially has a claim of action. It should be noted that the absence of a covenant not to compete or a specific agreement not to disclose or use trade secrets in and of itself does not prove the absence of a trade secret given that other "reasonable measures" were taken to insure the secrecy of the information.

Although the use of a nondisclosure agreement is recommended as part of a strategic protection effort, it must be emphasized that the UTSA does not require the use of a nondisclosure agreement for information to qualify as a trade secret, only that a firm exert reasonable efforts to maintain the information's secrecy. Despite not having an express, restrictive covenant in place, it was noted that Fleming apparently had taken several reasonable steps to insure the secrecy of the information. Persons to whom the information was entrusted were advised to preserve the confidentiality of the information. Additionally, the firm's operating policies manual contained a proviso that an employee was subject to termination for revealing confidential information belonging to the firm. The court apparently was not bothered by the assertion that the information sometimes was kept in the offices of sales representatives in an unlocked environment, noting that such information normally is available to sales representatives and to preclude such dissemination would serve to prevent the firm from conducting its business affairs. Given the facts that the firm limited the dissemination of the information to a need-to-know basis, that advisories to maintain confidentiality were given to those to whom access was provided, and that other security steps had been taken by the firm, one might conclude that reasonable efforts had been taken to protect the information.

It should be emphasized that, in this case, there was no allegation that Bailey had taken a customer "list" from the firm. The charges grew from the fact that Bailey had intimate knowledge of the customer list and the information it contained and was using such information and knowledge in his new employ. Purportedly, the new firm was charged as being able to gain a similar competitive advantage from the knowledge base of its sales force, some of whom were former sales representatives of Fleming who also were privy to the confidential customer information claimed by Fleming as a trade secret.

A telling issue was the possibility that the information construed to be trade secrets was readily available from other sources. If the information in question was the subject of reasonable efforts to maintain its secrecy but the information was readily available in the public domain, it would not qualify as a trade secret under the auspices of the UTSA. Testimony revealed that the names of firms in the industry and information as to the principals of those firms could be obtained, in many instances, from the phone book and in a trade directory that compiled the information and made it available to those in the industry. The court noted that an argument as to the completeness of a customer list developed from these sources may not mirror exactly the customer list of Fleming, but substantial amounts of the information in the list could be ascertained from these sources. The court felt it would be unreasonable to construe the "readily ascertainable" standard as specified in the act as requiring an exact duplicate of information claimed to be a trade secret and, therefore, found that the knowledge that Bailey (and his sales force) possessed of the industry did not constitute a trade secret belonging to Fleming.

Further, information as to customers and their requirements acquired through the normal efforts of sales representatives comprises information that may be "readily ascertainable through proper means." Skills and knowledge acquired in the course of employment that become a part of the general knowledge base of an employee potentially comprises that which an employee is free to take and use in other pursuits. This is especially true in situations in which a valid restrictive covenant is shown not to exist. In the absence of an allegation that a former employee removed a physical listing of customer information and in the absence of a restrictive covenant, a charge that the former employee is misappropriating trade secrets, which one may consider a part of the individual's general knowledge base, would be difficult, if not impossible, to support.

A manufacturer of transport systems that incorporated vibrating technology to move machine parts of various shapes and sizes along a production line to specific locations within a production environment sued a firm established by some of its former employees. The manufacturer claimed that the new firm misappropriated its trade secrets in developing its customer list. In the case of *Xpert Automation Systems, Corporation v. Vibromatic Company, Inc.*, the manufacturer, Vibromatic, undoubtedly was disappointed that Indiana's Fifth District Court of Appeals reversed a lower court ruling that had found that its customer list was a trade secret. In finding that the customer list in this case was not a trade secret under Indiana's UTSA, the court of appeals differentiated between having knowledge of customers and having a list of customers.

Xpert Automation's principal employees previously had held responsible positions at Vibromatic, having worked for varying lengths of time ranging from seven years to 22 years. While at Vibromatic, the individuals had become acquainted with some of that firm's customers and, not surprisingly, had developed personal relationships with several. In addition, while employed, the individuals were privy to the computer data base containing customer information. Vibromatic reportedly had several security measures in place aimed at protecting its customer list. The list was kept in a computer data base that had access security. The computer disk containing the customer data base was the subject of reasonable security efforts, and only the two former employees, now among Xpert's principal employees, were allowed access to the customer data base. In addition, Vibromatic claimed that its list had been developed over time and that it contained the names of good customers, contending that problem customers had been eliminated from its list over time.

Shortly after leaving the employ of Vibromatic, the individuals involved established Xpert Automation Systems. Among the customers Xpert solicited were customers of Vibromatic. Indeed, as the trial revealed, some 200 of Vibromatic's customers were among the names of over 500 prospective customers Xpert apparently planned to target. Xpert claimed that, in addition to market knowledge, it used a variety of sources to develop its data base, including customer referrals and cold calling on individuals in production environments.

The trial court found that the customer list of Vibromatic qualified as a trade secret. Further, the inclusion of over 200 Vibromatic customers on Xpert's list resulted in the conclusion that Vibromatic's secrets had been misappropriated. Xpert appealed the decision on several grounds, especially on the basis of a perceived error in the court's recognition of the list as a trade secret. The court of appeals reversed the finding that the list was a trade secret.

Citing the UTSA, the court noted that a trade secret is information that "derives independent economic value, actual or potential from not being generally known to, and not being readily ascertainable by proper means by other persons who can obtain economic value from its disclosure or use." The phrase, "not being readily ascertainable by proper means" provides the key to understanding the reversal. The trial court found that cold calling the names in a noted industry directory was less efficient, more time consuming, and more costly than working with a list of customers with whom a relationship has already been established. This finding was a major factor in the reversal. If the names of the potential customers can be discovered in a trade directory, even if it is somewhat more difficult than having a previously established and purged list, the names still are ascertainable in a relatively inexpensive fashion by proper means. Thus, even given extensive security measures to maintain the confidentiality of any information, the information does not qualify as a trade secret if it can be readily ascertained by proper means. As one might surmise from this discussion, the preliminary injunction issued by the trial court that prohibited Xpert from soliciting or accepting business from customers of Vibromatic was overturned.

As one may further surmise, many firms currently are requiring employees to sign nondisclosure, noncompetition agreements that forbid the future use or disclosure of a firm's trade secret information. By themselves, do such agreements provide the atmosphere of confidentiality that will preclude misappropriations of trade secrets by those to whom such information is entrusted? Does a firm that incorporates a nondisclosure, noncompetition agreement as a part of its employment process always have the upper hand in a case alleging misappropriation by an employee or former employee? The answer to both of these questions is a resounding no.

An employee agreement that prohibits nondisclosure or use of trade secret information will, probably, not establish by and of itself an atmosphere of confidentiality. Worse, such agreements are not always sufficient to prohibit the use or disclosure of such information. However, despite not being totally conclusive as to the existence of trade secrets in a given work environment, their use appears warranted. Just remember, by themselves, nondisclosure agreements may not accomplish what one might hope. It is important that they are specific as to which information the employee is expected not to disclose.

A case in point is *Electro-Craft Corporation v. Controlled Motion, Incorporated.* In this case, the Minnesota Supreme Court indicated that the mere signing of a nondisclosure agreement does not always provide the protection sought under the UTSA. The court held that the plaintiff had not proven the existence of a trade secret because of its failure to make reasonable efforts to maintain the secrecy of its process. Even though Electro-Craft required employees to sign an employment agreement that included a confidentiality provision (but not a noncompetition provision), the court held that the agreement was too vague to apprise the employees as to what specific information the firm considered to be secret. It also was noted that confidentiality and security procedures were lax; cited as examples were procedures that allowed motor diagrams the firm considered to be among its trade secrets to be routinely thrown away, rather than destroyed, and the fact that its technical documents were not marked as being or containing confidential information. As Electro-Craft discovered, an atmosphere of confidentiality that promulgates and expects that proprietary secrets of the firm are to be adequately safeguarded must be in place in order to gain protection of the UTSA.

One last benefit of analyzing and discerning which information a firm possesses for which it desires legal protection is that it allows for the thoughtful consideration by a firm's management as to which type of protection scheme would be most appropriate, given the information's vulnerability to outside discovery by competitors using proper and legal means. Patent protection or copyright protection may be better suited to provide legal protection for intellectual properties in certain situations. As may be surmised in the findings of a relevant case such as *Sheets v. Yamaha Motors Corporation, U.S.A.*, the timely patenting of items that are to be publicly displayed may provide the only effective form of protection for such proprietary property, because a public display is likely to remove any attempt at protection through the UTSA.

SUMMARY OF CONCEPTS

1. Information construed to be trade secrets needs to be delineated.
2. Reasonable efforts to maintain secrecy, given the circumstances, are expected.
3. Contractual agreements need to be specific as to which information a firm considers to be a trade secret.
4. Skills and knowledge acquired in the course of employment that are part of one's general knowledge potentially comprise that which an employee is free to take and use in other pursuits.
5. Restrictive contracts that are vague as to which information is considered secret will not be enforceable.

APPENDIX: CITATIONS AND MANAGEMENT IMPLICATIONS

Electro-Craft Corporation v. Controlled Motion, Incorporated et al. 332 N.W.2d 890 (Minn. 1983) — Confidentiality agreements must be specific as to which information is secret. Destroy surplus copies of secret documents; do not throw them away in the trash.

Gordon Employment Inc. v. Jewell 356 N.W.2d 738 (Minn.App. 1984) — Restrict access to secrets. Keep them secure when not in use. Treat valuable information as one would expect valuable information to be treated.

Nationwide Mutual Insurance Company v. Stenger 695 F.Supp. 688 (D.Conn. 1988) — Files containing secrets need to be protected. Labeling files as "confidential" may be a reasonable expectation. Label and protect both paper and computer files as containing secrets.

Fleming Sales Company, Inc. v. Bailey 611 F.Supp. 507 (D.C.Ill. 1985) — A nondisclosure agreement is not a requirement to prove secrecy. Reasonable efforts are necessary to maintain secrecy. Nondisclosure agreements are not required. General knowledge does not comprise a trade secret.

Xpert Automation Systems, Corporation v. Vibromatic Company, Inc. 569 N.E.2d 351 (Ind.App. 5 Dist. 1991) — A customer list that can be ascertained readily through proper means does not qualify as a trade secret.

Sheets v. Yamaha Motors Corporation, U.S.A. 849 F.2d 179 (5th Cir. 1988) — Reasonable efforts to maintain secrecy need to be made. Disclosing the secret to others negates the protectable nature of the information.

5

Appraising the Value of the Information

Without a doubt, the majority of cases involving the Uniform Trade Secrets Act (UTSA) that have been adjudicated since the act's development and recommendation to the states have revolved around either the issue of value of the information in dispute or the issue of secrecy of the information, with the issue of secrecy arising more often and in more cases than the issue of value. The UTSA defines a trade secret as being "information, including a formula, pattern, compilation, program, device, method, technique, or process, that derives independent economic value, actual or potential, from not being generally known to, and not being readily ascertainable by proper means by, other persons who can obtain economic value from its disclosure or use, and is the subject of efforts that are reasonable under the circumstances to maintain its secrecy." If the information in question is viewed as having no value, or is held to not be secret due to insufficiency in the steps taken to protect and maintain its secrecy, then the information in question is not a trade secret and as such will not garner protection support from the courts.

In determining value, factors that may be considered by the courts were delineated in the case of *SI Handling Systems, Inc. v. Heisley*. These factors include "the value of the information to the owner and his or her competitors, the amount of effort or money expended by the owner in developing the information, and the ease or difficulty with which the information could be properly acquired or duplicated by others." The

UTSA does not spell out how much value information is expected to have in order for it to be protected under its provisions, but the courts have taken the position that the information should have significant value in order to meet the value expectation of a trade secret. An expectation of significant value raises questions as to value sufficiency, and, as a result, the question has been broached in more than one case.

In *Templeton v. Creative Loafing Tampa, Inc.*, the District Court of Appeal of Florida, Second District, reversed a lower court ruling that awarded a magazine publisher damages and injunctive relief under the UTSA. The magazine had sought damages and injunctive relief against a former employee, alleging that the employee was using confidential information obtained from lists that were considered trade secrets belonging to the firm (Creative Loafing Tampa, Inc.). As noted, the lower court found for the magazine publisher. However, the appeals court overturned the decision, basing part of its finding on the issue of value.

The confidential information in dispute was composed of advertiser and distribution lists for a magazine published by the firm. The lists had been developed over several years by the previous publisher of the magazine during the course of business. The lists supposedly contained the names of potential advertisers, the names and addresses of potential distribution outlets, primary contact information, and other relevant information. Copies of the magazines were distributed free of charge to the public at various commercial business locations whose managers had agreed to allow such distribution.

Creative Loafing Tampa, Inc., purchased the magazine and its associated goodwill from its previous owner, for whom Templeton had worked for approximately eight years. Shortly after the sale of the magazine to Creative Loafing Tampa, Templeton left the employ of the magazine with the intent of starting a competitive publication. Templeton is said to have had in his possession, at the time he parted, copies of advertiser and distribution lists. Within a few days, though, he voluntarily returned the lists.

Within two weeks of leaving, Templeton published the first issue of his competitive magazine. It was charged that most of the advertisers in Templeton's magazine were among those advertising in the magazine purchased by Creative Loafing Tampa, Inc. In addition, the upstart magazine was being distributed in many of the same locations as the original.

Shortly thereafter, Creative Loafing Tampa, Inc., filed suit, seeking damages and injunctive relief for the unauthorized use of information contained in the lists, which the firm considered to be among its trade secrets. The trial court found for Creative Loafing Tampa, noting that the firm had suffered irreparable harm by the actions of Templeton, partly because of his use of the firm's trade secrets. The trial court enjoined Templeton from using the information contained in the lists in his business pursuits. Specifically, he was enjoined from contacting or soliciting advertisers and potential distributors whose names and contact information appeared on the lists.

Templeton appealed the decision. The appeals court overturned the trial court's decision and removed the injunction, finding that the lists in question did not qualify as trade secrets. The question of value was among the items of interest in the appeals process. The appellate court noted that the lists of potential advertisers for the magazine and potential distributors did not qualify as trade secrets because the lists were not a product of great expense or effort, they were distillations of larger lists, and they did not include information not readily available from public sources. The court noted that a list of potential advertisers for such a publication can be ascertained readily by anyone who would scan previous issues of the original magazine, taking note of which firms had been placing advertisements in the publication. The appeals court noted that there was no secret as to the identity of potential advertisers and distributors, all of whom comprise a readily ascertainable group.

Regarding the distributor listing, the court found that no great effort was needed to ascertain the business names on the listing. It was noted that one could follow the firm's delivery truck and note the addresses of drop-off points. As for determining optimal quantities to drop off at each location, a potential claim to show effort and expertise in the course of such a business pursuit, the court noted that no significant expertise or significant levels of common sense were needed to estimate how much to drop off at any one location. It can be surmised that a simple trial would indicate whether more or fewer copies of the magazine needed to be dropped off at any one location, a relatively easy and inexpensive proposition.

The court noted that the names of the contacts at the firms purchasing advertising from the magazine potentially constituted the only secret information on the advertiser list. Templeton's testimony indicated he knew the contact parties personally and did not need the list to ascertain their names. Therefore, the court found that Templeton could not be precluded from utilizing contacts and expertise gained during the term of his previous employment.

An interesting point surfaced in the case concerning noncompetition and confidentiality agreements. There were none. Templeton had never entered into a covenant not to compete with either Tampa Creative Loafing or with the previous owner of the magazine. Therefore, the court could not find that Templeton had breached any contractual obligations not to disclose the information to others or to make use of the information. Further, it was noted that Templeton had no ownership interest in the original magazine and, so, could not be perceived as being in a position of impairing the goodwill of the firm as purchased by the magazine's new owner.

In summary, the appeals court ruled that the advertiser and distribution lists were not trade secrets under the UTSA because no great effort or expense had been involved in their preparation, they were not distillations of larger lists, and the information was readily available to those willing to expend minimal effort. Because no trade secrets were found to be in dispute, no injunction forbidding their use logically could ensue. The appeals court found that Templeton was within his right to use the information at his disposal. Remember, if an owner or plaintiff fails to show that the information has value, the information will not be protected under the UTSA.

American Credit Indemnity Company v. Sacks was another case involving the question of value related to a customer list, and the court's final outcome was more in line with what the plaintiff firm wanted to hear. Sacks had been an agent for American Credit Indemnity Company for approximately nine years. American Credit Indemnity is engaged in the credit insurance business, selling credit insurance to a host of firms who utilize their own credit accounts in the course of their businesses. Reportedly, American Credit Indemnity is one of three major competitors in the industry, staffing over 42 offices and generating gross premiums exceeding $56 million annually. The industry is competitively challenging, because it was reported that only about 6.5 percent of firms who could utilize credit insurers to reduce risks associated with their financing portfolios actually do so.

Toward the end of her employment at American Credit Indemnity, Sacks decided to leave that firm and open an independent insurance agency that represented Fidelity and Deposit Company of Maryland. Fidelity and Deposit was a competitor of American Credit Indemnity. Through her new agency, Sacks was engaged in selling the credit insurance products of Fidelity and Deposit. Three days after resigning, Sacks sent a letter to the policyholders she had serviced at American Credit Indemnity, announcing her establishment of an independent agency and her representation of Fidelity and Deposit. Although the announcement did state that American Credit would continue to service their accounts, an offer was made in the announcement for Sacks to discuss the Fidelity and Deposit products in detail and to review the customer's insurance needs at renewal time. Sacks also admitted to calling each of the individuals who had received the announcement letter to convey a personal communication of departure but denied that the calls were made to solicit business or to discourage the parties contacted from continuing their policies with American Credit Indemnity.

Shortly thereafter, American Credit Indemnity filed suit, seeking, among other things, an injunction that would prevent Sacks from utilizing its trade secrets, including its customer list, policy expiration dates, lists of all leads for potential sales, claims histories, and other information related to the special needs of its customers. Although the trial court found that monetary damages provided an adequate remedy for American Credit Indemnity's unfair competition claim, it did not find that the evidence supported the claim for misappropriation of trade secrets. Specifically, the trial court did not recognize the customer list as a trade secret belonging exclusively to American Credit.

Testimony revealed that American Credit Indemnity had taken steps to ensure and maintain secrecy relative to its client list and related information the firm considered a trade secret. The firm purportedly had an employee confidentiality agreement that required employees to recognize and agree not to use or disclose the firm's secrets. However, Sacks denied ever signing such an agreement. Further, it was noted that Sacks, while an employee, had access to the names of approximately 3,000 leads and clients maintained by American Credit Indemnity pursuant to the discovery process in another suit in which she claimed defamation by a former secretary of the firm. Relative to the receipt of those materials in the other case, Sacks and others involved had stipulated to a protective order covering the information. In other words, all parties agreed that the logbooks containing the information on leads and clients were proprietary and confidential information belonging to American Credit Indemnity. Further, the parties in that suit and their representatives agreed that the information divulged in the books could be used only for the purposes of the litigation at hand and that the material was not to be disclosed, discussed, copied, published, or otherwise made available to anyone other than the parties involved, their counsels, and those with a legitimate need to know in order to assist in the prosecution or defense of that action.

In short, American Credit Indemnity contended that its customer list, policy expiration dates, and related information were trade secrets belonging to it. The firm charged its former employee with misappropriating its trade secrets by soliciting its customers using proprietary information for which it had provided reasonable protection. Among the remedies sought,

American Credit Indemnity sought an injunction to prevent further use of its client list by its former employee.

Contrary to the findings of the trial court, the court of appeal found that the customer list in contention was information that derived independent economic value from not being generally known and was the subject of reasonable efforts to maintain its secrecy; as such, its use should have been enjoined. Thus, it met the two-prong test as to whether information constitutes a trade secret under the UTSA. The unique nature of the credit insurance business and the sales resistance that must be overcome to underwrite such policies were perceived as imparting significant economic value to the information. Further, although the court noted that the right to enter and announce new business affiliations has not been diminished by the enactment of the UTSA, the announcement letter sent by Sacks was construed as going beyond an appropriate professional announcement and constituted a solicitation of American Credit Indemnity's customers. Such a solicitation was found to be a misappropriation of American Credit Indemnity's trade secrets. The court of appeals found that enjoining further unfair competition was appropriate, given the evidence in the case.

So, value is seen as one of the major factors in delineating whether or not an item of information may be construed to be a trade secret. To be a trade secret, the secret must possess significant, independent economic value from which its owner derives benefit. For many trade secrets, the value of the information may be easy to calculate. In such cases, showing value may be a matter of having good cost accounting information available from which actual costs associated with the information may be derived. For still other trade secrets, the ability of items to add to the bottom lines in their specific competitive environments may be the key to demonstrating value. In still other situations, the notion of value may be difficult to demonstrate. For instance, what happens if the information one possesses and construes to be a trade secret has no direct value, but for competitors to avail themselves of the information, they would have to invest a substantial sum of money or effort? For those possessing such secrets, the commissioners were equally diligent in recognizing the need to provide for their protection.

An interesting corollary to the notion of having value under the UTSA is the idea of having value from a negative point of view. The fact that the list had been developed over some time by weeding out potential noncustomers relates to the concept of value from a negative viewpoint. The names of businesses that are not really interested in using the services of temporary employment agencies is valuable — perhaps in a negative sense, but still valuable. In other words, for others to discern the names of firms not likely to purchase the services of an employment agency, time, effort, and expense would have to be entailed.

The commissioners' comments accompanying the act include an interesting corollary to "having value," namely, the concept of having a "value from a negative viewpoint." In a business context, one can envision a situation in which a firm invests a substantial sum of money to test market a new product. The new product test marketing and attendant data collection and analysis process indicate to the testing firm that the product would be a costly failure if the marketer were to pursue mass distribution of the product. Information relating to the potential for failure of this project could permit competitors to bypass such a data collection and marketing approach, potentially saving the competing firm substantial sums of money. As a result, the knowledge that the product did not pan out in the test marketing process is valuable to the holder of the knowledge. In such a situation, the knowledge is valuable, but the value arises in a reverse or negative connotation. Such value, even in a negative sense, still comprises the concept of value under the intent of the UTSA.

Similarly, one may find that a firm has purchased an expensive prospect list from a third-party list provider but subsequently found the list to be largely unsuitable for use in its competitive environment. Additional significant effort and expense are undertaken by the purchasing firm to cull the list and identify the few individuals or firms on the list that are true prospects for the firm's products. Once again, competitors who could obtain the true prospect information without the expense or effort of purchasing and culling the master list would reap significant benefits from the knowledge of the individuals or firms on the list that are not seen to be potential customers for the industry's product. The time, expense, and effort to weed out noncustomers from the population of all businesses give value to those who are in the know. In such a case, one has information of value — negative value, to be sure, but valuable information nonetheless.

One may note a firm that expends substantial funds and effort to determine the optimal site location at which to build a new branch. In so doing, the firm entails significant expense in determining which sites would not be potentially good locations. For a competitor to obtain the information discerning which sites of several under consideration are likely to be poorly performing sites, it would have to invest similar effort and go to similar expense to weed out the bad locations. On the other hand, if it could surreptitiously find out which sites do not hold promise by misappropriating the information from the first firm, the potential for trade secrets misappropriation exists. In other words, the knowledge of which sites would be poor performers possesses value — negative value perhaps, but value. The potential existence of negative value is recognized in the implementation of the UTSA.

In sum, if the information that is desired to be protected has no independent economic value, then it cannot be protected under the provisions of the UTSA. If it has value, it may be eligible for protection under the UTSA. Information with value from a negative perspective does possess value and, therefore, may be construed to be a trade secret under the provisions of the UTSA. The UTSA protects secret information of value for which adequate security has been provided.

SUMMARY OF CONCEPTS

1. The UTSA offers protection for secret information that has value.
2. Courts expect that protectable secrets will have significant value.
3. Easily obtainable information that costs little has no value under the provisions of the UTSA.
4. Value can be defined in a negative sense and can impart trade secret status on information that contains such value.

APPENDIX: CITATIONS AND MANAGEMENT IMPLICATIONS

SI Handling Systems, Inc. v. Heisley 753 F.2d. 1244 (1985) — Information to be protected must have significant value for the UTSA to apply.

Templeton v. Creative Loafing Tampa, Inc. 552 So.2d 288 (Fla.App. 2 Dist. 1989) — Trade secrets must have value. Information that is readily available and that costs little lacks value under the provisions of the UTSA.

American Credit Indemnity Company v. Sacks 262 Cal.Rptr. 92 (Cal.App. 2 Dist. 1989) — Specific, clear confidentiality agreements can play an important role in the secrecy maintenance process.

6

Appraising the Secrecy of the Information

Assuming that the information is deemed to have value, the next step in strategic analysis involves a determination as to whether the information of concern is, in fact, secret. To be eligible for Uniform Trade Secrets Act (UTSA) protection, the information must be secret and generally not known or legally knowable by others who can benefit from the knowledge to the detriment of the owner. As the commissioners point out in their comments to the act, information that is general knowledge to those in the industry cannot be protected under the UTSA, because the information is not a secret. Similarly, information that can be ascertained legally and readily by others is not eligible for UTSA protection. The information inherently must be a secret and its specifics not easily and legally ascertained.

If, for example, it is widely known within an industry that a particular prospect list being marketed as containing the names and addresses of suitable sales prospects for the products sold in the industry contains substantial erroneous information and lacks appropriate, useful market information for the industry, such knowledge, even though it may possess negative value, would not receive protection from the UTSA, because it is generally known. It is not a secret and, as a result, cannot be protected under the provisions of the UTSA. Similarly, if the information was available in a published article, the yellow pages, or other public sources, it would not be eligible for protection even if not widely known, because it is easily and legally ascertainable. Of course, if the owner of the information willingly shares the information with others and fails to take reasonable steps to insure its secrecy, the information will not be deemed to be a trade secret.

In *Sheets v. Yamaha Motors Corporation, U.S.A.*, it was seen that, if one willfully permits others to see and photograph an item that may be construed by some to be a trade secret, the potential for protection under the provisions of the UTSA is likely to be negated. Sheets' actions in allowing Yamaha representatives to view his alterations, in allowing his sons and their racing team to publicly race motorcycles containing the alterations, and in his giving what the court construed to be minimal instructions on the necessity of preserving the secrecy of the alterations to those in receipt of it were all seen as lacking in reasonableness relative to making a case that the device and attendant alterations were a secret. The courts have not been vague in assessing whether or not information is secret under the provisions of the UTSA. If information is secret, has independent economic value, and is subject to reasonable steps to insure its secrecy, it is likely to be seen as a secret. If not, then secrecy is lacking, as is any legitimate hope that a court will recognize the information as secret.

A purchaser of patents, patent applications, designs, and trade secrets related to oil tools became enmeshed in legal proceedings when the purchaser charged the seller with committing a breach of contract relating to the agreement in which the patents and trade secrets in question were sold. The contract covering the sale stipulated that the purchaser would receive assistance from the seller in the form of management counseling in its research and development activities, patent application efforts, and the engineering process related to the production of the tools. As a part of its reply to the charges, the selling firm filed a reconventional demand seeking monetary damages and the recovery of the items and trade secrets surrendered in the sales transaction. The seller alleged that a payment schedule as contained in the purchase contract had not been followed. At the trial court level, a variety of problems plagued the legal process prior to the trial proceedings, including the fact that the plaintiff's counsel withdrew from the case only four days prior to the scheduled trial date. On withdrawing from the case, the plaintiff's attorney requested that a continuance be granted in order to allow his client time to retain counsel and to provide the new counsel with sufficient time to adequately prepare for the case. The trial court refused, and the trial ensued as scheduled.

In that case, *Razorback Oil Tools International, Inc. v. Taylor Oil Tools Company*, a question as to the existence and ownership of trade secrets bore on the decision that granted the plaintiff's request for a new trial. The court of appeal, in hearing the request, noted that sufficient grounds existed that should have resulted in an affirmative decision to grant the trial continuance. Specifically, the withdrawal of the plaintiff's counsel on short notice and a question as to whether certain legal documents had been served adequately were seen as major hindrances to the fair disposition of the case. Additionally, it found that the judgment contained errors that undermined the integrity of the awarding of a sizeable sum of money (some $15 million) on the reconventional demand. In its deliberations concerning the errors in the judgment, the question of whether a trade secret can be recovered was addressed.

The question addressed by the court concerns whether or not one who sells a trade secret and who then finds himself or herself in a situation in which the buyer fails to pay for the secret as contracted can recover the secret and maintain it again as its own secret? The question begged to be answered, because $6 million of the judgment was for compensatory and punitive damages related to trade secrets violations. The court of appeal addressed this question in its judgment, which ordered a new trial. The court noted that the seller voluntarily revealed his secrets to the buyer as a part of the purchase transaction. As can be surmised, even without adequate payment, the secret has been revealed. A charge that the buyer had or had not paid his obligations did not remove the fact that the secrets had been surrendered voluntarily. The court could not infer that the buyer's actions were a violation of Louisiana's version of the UTSA. Accordingly, the court of appeal ordered a new trial on all issues.

A case involving a temporary employment service that accused former employees of misappropriating trade secrets provides additional insight into the role of customer lists in the trade secrets arena. In *Courtesy Temporary Service, Inc. v. Camacho et al.*, the plaintiff firm accused three former employees of misappropriation of trade secrets. It was charged that the three former employees left the employ of Courtesy and started their own temporary employment service. The three purportedly used confidential customer information that had been obtained through and during their association with Courtesy to begin and operate their competing firm.

Further, it was purported that Camacho and others obtained a confidential customer list, pricing and profit information, customer requirements, and other proprietary information belonging to Courtesy and used it for the purpose of starting and running a competing firm. The superior court, citing a case in which a customer list was not found to be a trade secret, did not enjoin Camacho and the new firm from utilizing the information they had obtained while in the employ of Courtesy. The court of appeal overturned the lower court finding and noted that the customer list in question was a trade secret capable of being protected by the UTSA. The court noted that the list had been developed by Courtesy over several years, requiring ingenuity, time, labor, and expense. The list and related information also had been subject to a variety of security measures.

In the case of *Abba Rubber Company v. Seaquist et al.*, the question arose as to whether customer lists are considered to be trade secrets. The record reveals that, in this case, former employees of Abba subsequently went to work for the Seaquist Company, a competitive rubber roller operation started by the original principal of Abba. Seaquist entered the rubber roller business after a noncompetition clause, executed when Abba was sold, expired.

For the five years between the sale of Abba by its founder and the entrance of Seaquist into the rubber roller market, Seaquist was engaged in the metal fabrication business. It began making rubber roller products and entered the market as a competitor of Abba, though, supposedly, it had no sales force specific to the rubber roller market, nor did it significantly expand its operation in that area.

Approximately four years later, Seaquist hired two brothers who had worked previously for Abba. Although one of the brothers had just departed Abba's employ, the other had worked more recently for another rubber roller company. The firm began to expand its rubber roller operation, leasing a new building to anchor its rubber operations and assigning one of the brothers specifically to sell in that market. Shortly thereafter, Abba filed suit, claiming, among other things, that its trade secrets had been misappropriated. The suit asked for preliminary and permanent injunctive relief and, of course, damages.

The brothers denied taking any customer records from Abba. They did admit to soliciting Abba's customers by means of a mailing announcing the relocation and association of one of the brothers to Seaquist. Individuals receiving the solicitation were advised as to how to contact the brother for price, quality, and service.

The California court found that the customer list was a trade secret according to California's version of the UTSA. In reading the UTSA, one notes that secret information must not be generally known to the public or to other persons who can obtain economic value from its disclosure or use. Thus, the information must be valuable and secret. The court noted that knowledge of businesses that purchase products from a particular firm is of no particular value to competitors unless the information indicates a fact they did not know, namely, that the businesses listed use goods or services that the competitors market. Thus, a customer list may contain secret information for which adequate protection has been provided and harbor significant value, which may qualify the list as a trade secret.

However, it should be noted this case was filed and prosecuted under California's version of the UTSA. Because California's version of the UTSA deleted a specific phrase as implemented in other states' statutes, a further look at the case and additional explanation is warranted. In this case, the defendants argued that the identity of firms that constituted the consumers of rubber rollers should fail to meet the definition of a trade secret because the identities were "readily ascertainable" and, thus, could not be construed to be trade secrets. Specifically, they claimed that the identities of potential customers for rubber roller products were readily available and revealed in a variety of outlets, including trade directories, telephone books, and other public sources of information. Therefore, they argued that the list should not be considered a trade secret.

In the specific wording of the UTSA, it can be seen that trade secrets are referred to as information that derives independent economic value, actual or potential, from not being generally known to, *and not being readily ascertainable by proper means by*, other persons who can obtain economic value from its disclosure or use. However, California's legislature did not include the italicized phrase in its trade secrets legislation prior to the adoption of its version of the UTSA. Therefore, a potential exists for cases being heard in California resulting in slightly different outcomes than cases filed in those states that adopted the wording as prescribed by the commissioners. It can be surmised that the California legislature was reacting apparently to the concern of some that inclusion of the phrase would cloud the definition of a trade secret and invite speculation and litigation concerning the definition of a trade secret. The result of the implementation under California's wording of the law is that information can be a trade secret even though it is readily ascertainable by third parties. To qualify as a trade secret in California, the secret information may be readily ascertainable, but it must not have been ascertained by others in the industry at the time of contention or misappropriation. California's statutory intent is to punish the wrongful acquisition of information, even if the information could have been obtained legally.

IMI-Tech v. Gagliani et al., as already discussed in Chapter 3, was another California-based case in which that state's trade secrets statute's exclusion of the stipulation that a secret "not be readily ascertainable by proper means by others" became a point of consideration by the court. IMI-Tech's case revolved around its allegation that Gagliani had misappropriated its process used in the manufacture of a fire resistant foam. A part of Gagliani's argument centered around the potential for others, primarily government agencies, to have had access to the information on which the process was based. The potential that someone could have ascertained the process did nothing to diminish IMI-Tech's arguments that no one had ascertained the process and that the secrecy of the process had been maintained. Again, California's version of the UTSA has a small but potentially important difference as implemented compared with the UTSA as adopted by most states. Still, whether one is in California or not, it is the intent of the act to discourage the misappropriation of trade secrets and provide remedy for those whose secrets have been unjustly exploited.

Another case involving a personnel placement firm and one of its former employees accused of using its customer list saw the plaintiff firm fail in its attempt to convince the court that it possessed trade secrets that had been misappropriated. In *Gordon Employment, Inc. v. Jewell*, the employment agency sued Jewell after she left the employ of Gordon and started her own employment agency. The agency charged misappropriation of trade secrets. It claimed that Jewell had taken and was using its proprietary customer list. Unfortunately for Gordon, the court held that the list did not constitute a trade secret under the UTSA. The court noted that the employment agency had made no effort to keep the list confidential. It was reported that the list was kept in an unlocked file cabinet situated in a public reception area. The folder containing the list was not labeled "confidential," nor were the file cabinets. In addition, Gordon had no written policy regarding the confidentiality of the information or providing in any way for its security. If information is not secret, then the UTSA cannot and will not protect it. If it is secret, reasonable steps to insure its continued secrecy need to be taken by the firm's management.

Information that can be readily and legally known to competitors through reverse engineering or other lawful efforts cannot be protected under the UTSA. In *Acuson Corporation v. Aloka Company, LTD.*, it was seen that legally acquired products that are the target of reverse engineering efforts are not eligible for UTSA protection. Acuson's suit against Aloka alleged misappropriation of trade secrets and centered around the potential for discovery of the firm's trade secrets through reverse engineering of one of its products.

Acuson, a manufacturer of ultrasonic imaging equipment headquartered in Delaware, charged Aloka, a Japanese firm, with misappropriation of its trade secrets. Aloka admitted purchasing an Acuson product and claimed that the reason it made the purchase was to compare it with its own competing product. Acuson charged that the real reason behind Aloka's purchase of the product was a plan to copy the product and, as a result, place Aloka in a position of being able to use Acuson's technology against Acuson. Acuson emphasized that the manner in which Aloka acquired its product was, in its view, questionable and contributed to its belief that the purchase and subsequent reverse engineering by Aloka amounted to a misappropriation of trade secrets under the provisions of the UTSA.

Allegedly, Aloka did not acquire the Acuson product through a direct purchase from Acuson. Instead, Aloka asked its U.S. distributor to purchase the unit and requested that it be shipped to the firm's plant in Tokyo. The U.S. distributor purchased the device, service manuals, and a crate suitable for export from a medical equipment dealer with which it did business. Service manuals were included in the purchase because of a specific request by the equipment distributor acknowledging that the equipment would be exported and, thus, be beyond Acuson's service area. The product was delivered, and Aloka paid its distributor for the device in a timely manner, and, in turn, the distributor quickly paid the equipment firm. Acuson, though, did not receive payment from the equipment firm and sued to get the balance due on the order. Apparently, as a result, Acuson learned that the equipment had been purchased by Aloka. It dropped its suit for payment and demanded that the device be returned instead. Aloka refused to surrender the device. The suit seeking a preliminary injunction reportedly was filed approximately ten months after Acuson first learned that Aloka had obtained the device through the equipment firm. As requested by Acuson, a preliminary injunction was granted by the trial court.

Aloka posited four contentions in its effort to get the injunction vacated. First, it noted that Acuson's product could not contain trade secrets because hundreds had been sold on the open market. Second, Acuson failed to identify its trade secrets. Third, Acuson failed to satisfy certain traditional prerequisites for injunctive relief; specifically, the prerequisites Acuson is alleged to have failed to show included a probability of success on the merits of its case, the existence of irreparable harm to the plaintiff, and diligence in the sense that the suit was filed in a timely manner. The last contention posited by Aloka was the charge that the injunction was overly broad.

The court of appeal noted that each of Aloka's contentions had merit, but, to reach its decision, only the first contention had to be considered. Did Acuson's product contain trade secrets? As the court noted, that which constitutes a trade secret is a question of law, not a finding of fact. In its review of the case, the court focused on the question as to whether or not the facts supported the conclusion that a trade secret exists. If a secret is not shown to exist, then injunctive relief cannot properly ensue.

Information that is disclosed to the public cannot be construed to be a trade secret. Trade secrets that are disclosed to the public lose their secrecy and their potential for protection under the law after disclosure. In addition, as was noted by the court, state law may not prohibit the copying of objects that exist in the public domain. According to the UTSA, a trade secret is information that derives independent economic value "from not being generally known to the public or to other persons who can obtain economic value from its disclosure or use." The definition embodied in the act puts the onus on a secret's owner to ensure that reasonable steps are taken to prevent disclosure. If one desires protection under the UTSA, then one must keep the information secret. Specifically, information or products that have been disclosed publicly cannot be construed to be trade secrets eligible for protection under trade secrets law. The point of discourse needing to be addressed is whether or not Acuson disclosed its own secrets and, in doing so, gave up any claim to the secrets.

In this case, the court found that Acuson publicly disclosed its "secrets" through the sales of its machines. The court took the position that there can be no trade secrets in products that have been disclosed by sale to the public. Relative to the indirect manner in which Aloka had obtained the device, it was noted that the notion that a customer disguises its identity when involved in a legal purchase transaction does not give rise to a cause of action for misappropriation of trade secrets. Additionally, an Acuson claim that the product was not disclosed to the "general public" because only doctors and other health care providers comprised the market to which the firm's ultrasonic equipment was sold was not acceded to by the court. The language of the UTSA is clear in that the information should "not be generally known to the public or to other persons." It is not necessary that a secret be known to the public for trade secrets rights to be lost. If persons who can obtain economic advantages from the knowledge inherent in a trade secret are knowledgeable as to the information, then a trade secret no longer exists.

Another issue Acuson brought to bear in its charge of misappropriation concerned a confidentiality agreement that it required employees and dealers to sign concerning nondisclosure of information relative to the trade secrets the firm claimed were inherent in the machine's design and operation. Acuson argued that the use of the agreements was indicative of the reasonable efforts the firm had followed in trying to maintain its trade secrets. Although nondisclosure agreements may sustain the secrecy of information within a specific work environment, they cannot prevent the public acquisition or dissemination of secrets contained in products that have been sold on the open market. The court noted that, in view of the apparently wide distribution of the machine in the medical market, Acuson had not met expectations as to secrecy maintenance.

One last issue that deserves mention concerning Acuson's efforts to maintain the secrecy of its product was the existence of multiple padlocks placed within the product to prevent or discourage unauthorized servicing. Acuson's claim that Aloka had to break two of the locks in order for its engineers to complete their study of the machine was proffered as another instance of Aloka knowingly acting to misappropriate Acuson's secrets. The court noted that, in breaking the locks, Aloka was acting within its rights as owner of the machine, and the locks so contained, to do with the locks as it pleased. At any rate, the presence of the locks in the machine was not intended to nor could it prevent an owner of the machine from accessing the internal components of the machine. The locks, as well as all other parts of the machine that could be examined by outsiders, even those that were behind locked panels, were considered as accessible to its owners.

In short, by selling its products on the open market in relatively large numbers, Acuson lost any claim to trade secrets contained in the machines. The existence and use of confidentiality agreements with the firm's employees and with outside distributors of the products and the use of padlocks to discourage internal access and maintenance by purchasers do not lend themselves to the establishment of secrecy and its maintenance in products that have been disclosed or released to the public. The court's statement that nothing that can be disclosed through an examination of the machine can be considered a trade secret left little doubt as to the outcome, in which the preliminary injunction was not upheld.

As an aside, it would appear that the only avenue opened to Acuson to maintain proprietary rights for its secrets as present in the machine would have been to avail itself of federal patent law. Potentially, the patent approach could have prevented unauthorized use of the firm's secrets for 17 years had the firm obtained patents on the machine and its component parts. The U.S. Supreme Court recognized that trade secret law and federal patent law can coexist, because trade secret law does not confer monopoly rights to objects in the public domain. In situations in which an object is not protected by federal copyright or patent law and is in the public domain, state law cannot bar the copying of such a product. Indeed, the potential or likelihood that objects in the public domain may be copied through reverse engineering is seen as an incentive for inventors to try and meet the requirements of patentability under federal statutes and obtain the limited exclusivity offered through patent law.

In a similar vein, the court hearing *Haan Crafts Corporation v. Craft Masters, Inc.*, noted that "business ideas and products which have been introduced to the public are in the public domain and may be freely copied unless they are legally protected by registered trademark, patent or copyright." Feats of reverse engineering performed legally would negate the possibility of the UTSA offering protection to a firm for a so-called secret. Thus, unless the information is secret and is treated as such, the UTSA will not provide the protection that many seek in court.

The background to the *Haan Crafts* case is not unlike that of many other cases involving an allegation of trade secrets misappropriation by former employees. Haan Crafts Corporation is engaged in the design and construction of a variety of items. Its primary product line consists of sewing kits that allow buyers to create a variety of craft items easily, including stuffed items, such as animals and other figures, gym clothing, and gym bags. Its target market is composed of classroom teachers of home economics. It reaches its market through the publication and mail distribution of an advertising brochure detailing the kits.

Craft Masters is a competing firm that was initiated by a former controller of Haan Crafts. It, too, makes sewing kits and caters to the home economics instructors market. Similar to Haan Craft's promotional efforts, Craft Masters' promotional efforts include a brochure mailed to junior and senior high-school home economics teachers. In some cases, the products of Craft Masters are so similar to Haan Crafts' products as to be indistinguishable by a casual observer. At about the time Craft Masters began operations, it hired an employee of Haan Crafts who had served as a designer of sewing kits to serve in a similar capacity. Shortly thereafter, it hired two other Haan Crafts employees, one of whom worked part-time while in the final days of her employ at Haan Crafts. One of these two employees supposedly was prevented by the owner of Haan Crafts in her attempt to remove sewing patterns from the files. The employee claimed that the patterns belonged to her and were needed so that they might be added to her employment portfolio. She was not allowed to take the patterns, and she left.

Haan Crafts sued, listing a variety of claims, including copyright infringement, unfair competition, tortious interference with business, and, for the purposes of this discussion, violation of its trade secrets under the UTSA. The plaintiff sought a preliminary injunction prohibiting the defendant from pursuing any of its competitive business activities, essentially seeking to close down its business operations.

In the case, the plaintiff admitted that many of its own sewing kits were, themselves, copies of other firms' products. However, two of its sewing kits, specifically designed and developed by Haan Crafts, took on further meaning. These two, it was argued, were protected by copyright laws, because of their use in advertising, and, in the case of one of the kits, by trademark law, because it had become part of the firm's logo in its advertising brochure.

In any quest in which a preliminary injunction is sought, a plaintiff must show that it faces a threat or situation of irreparable harm without an adequate remedy at law, that there is some likelihood that it would be successful on the merits of its claims, that, on balancing harm among the parties, the relative harm weighs in favor of the court granting the injunction, and that the public interest is served by the granting of the injunction. The court will take into account the four factors when assessing whether or not an injunction should ensue by making a factual determination on the basis of a fair interpretation of the evidence presented and in accord with principled applications of the law.

In deciding this case, all of these factors weighed in the court's decision. The final decision was not to enjoin Craft Masters from engaging in all of its business operations. The fact that many of the designs in question were in the public domain entered into the decision, because items in the public domain may be copied freely unless protected by registered copyright, patent, or trademark. However, Craft Masters was enjoined from selling the two kits that Haan Crafts claimed infringed on its copyrights and trademark privileges. The court noted that the regular use of one of the completed kits' figures juxtaposed near the name of the firm in its ads may have given rise to a common-law trademark entitled to legal protection. Thus, Craft Masters was enjoined from producing only the two specific kits for which potential merit existed as to an infringement of copyright or trademark privileges.

Recently, a local university student came to me with a question as to how best to protect a piece of lawn ornamentation he had developed. He described the object and its construction, largely composed of shaped wooden pieces, cloth, and small fasteners. He had been selling the ornaments for over a year and had made a relatively nice return, given his investment in materials and time. He reported selling over 100 of the ornaments over the course of the past year, primarily to local homeowners. Could trade secrets law, especially the UTSA, be of help to him in preventing others from copying his design and selling similar products? Based on the findings in the *Acuson* and *Haan Crafts* cases and on general knowledge of trade secrets law, the apparent answer is no. The more than 100 ornaments that had been sold could now be considered in the public domain. The student-inventor had made no effort to keep anything relative to the item secret. Therefore, no secret inherent in their construction that could be ascertained by those purchasing the ornaments or those viewing the ornaments in area yards could be protected under trade secrets law. Anyone with the materials, tools, and woodworking know-how is free to copy the ornaments, given that the student had no other legal protection of the item pending or in effect.

Either copyright law or patent law may provide an avenue for protecting the item if application for such is made in a timely manner and such is granted. Whether or not the student will be entitled to protection under one of those federal statutes is a matter for him to pursue or not, as he desires. Given the short explanatory narrative the student presented on his ornament and the success of his selling the item from door to door, the likelihood that he would prevail in a trade secrets dispute filed under the UTSA appears nil. The ornament could be construed as being in the public domain and, in the absence of any other protection scheme, is potentially fair game for others who possess the tools, equipment, and woodworking skills necessary to make similar ornaments.

When reviewing cases that have included charges of trade secrets misappropriation, it is interesting to note the variety of businesses and industries in which questions of misappropriation have played a role. Indeed, some firms claiming misappropriation ply their trade in what may be described by some as specialized or rather narrow markets. It is, perhaps, the competitive nature found in these so-called niche markets that makes firms so intent on protecting their trade secrets, because to lose a trade secret and its competitive advantage in a small market may mean the difference between long-term success and failure. It is essential in any industry to provide for the adequate protection of trade secrets. In those industries or markets in which secrets are at the center of the firm's existence, such protective efforts become paramount.

Three individuals who were employed in the sales of water treatment chemicals found themselves the target of a suit by a former employer who charged they had misappropriated his firm's trade secrets. In *Wright Chemical Corporation v. Johnson et al.*, the purchaser of the firm for which the three individuals had previously worked sought a preliminary injunction against them, claiming that the three had misappropriated trade secrets belonging to the firm. The question as to whether the information in question was legally a trade secret deserving of protection was raised as a central point in the case. Obviously, if no trade secrets exist, then no misappropriation can occur.

In *Wright*, the background information indicates that the three defendants had worked for a chemical firm that sold water treatment products to industrial users. The three had signed confidentiality agreements that precluded them from revealing trade secrets belonging to the firm. The firm subsequently was purchased by Wright. A provision in the purchase agreement dictated that all employees of the purchased firm would have their positions terminated on the effective date of the sale. The day after the sale and official termination, certain employees, including Johnson and the other two defendants, were offered employment in the new firm. They accepted the employment offer and began work. They did not sign confidentiality agreements with Wright Chemical. As a consequence of their working, the defendants had access to a fact book that contained information on products and pricing and other information that could be construed to be proprietary. They never had access to the specific chemical formulas used in the manufacture of the products they sold. In fact, the formulas for the products were maintained on a confidential basis by the head of the firm's laboratory. The firm, both before the purchase and after, maintained security for all formulas related to the composition of its water treatment products. As a result of a perception by the defendants that compensation and benefits were lower than expected, the three left the employ of Wright less than one year later.

Johnson and the others went to work for a competing firm in the industry. Shortly after their going to work for the new firm, the firm began marketing water treatment products that competed directly with the products of Wright. An attempt to reverse engineer the chemical formulas of some of Wright's products was made through chemical analyses. The exact composition of the chemical formulas for Wright's product apparently was not ascertained or was inconsequential, as evidenced by the resulting products being chemically different from the original products subjected to the analyses. The new products that competed with Wright's products contained some of the same ingredients as Wright's, but not in the same quantity, and they contained chemicals not present in Wright's products. It was noted that none of the ingredients used in Wright's products were secret or exclusive to the Wright firm but were, instead, readily available from a variety of suppliers. The new firm began selling its products in direct competition with Wright. Wright sued and, among other contentions, claimed that the firm's trade secrets had been misappropriated. An injunction to restrain Johnson and the others from utilizing its trade secrets was sought.

The trial court held that the chemical formulas in question were trade secrets belonging to Wright. The climate of confidentiality surrounding their existence and use apparently was sufficient to delineate the formulas as trade secrets. The secrecy surrounding the formulas, their placement under the control of the head of the laboratory, and the specific nature of the chemicals and the maintenance of their composition on a confidential basis by both Wright and the previous firm apparently were deemed as being reasonable and sufficiently adequate to have the formulas declared trade secrets by the court. Once the question as to whether or not the chemical products were trade secrets was decided, the question that begged to be addressed was whether or not the firm's trade secrets had, in fact, been misappropriated.

Regarding the potential misappropriation of Wright's trade secrets, the court found no evidence to indicate that the three former employees actually disseminated the formulas or had in some way used them in the context of their new employment. Indeed, it appears in reviewing the case background that the three did not have access to the chemical formulas and, therefore, were not in a position to misappropriate them. Any information the new firm possessed with regard to the formulas apparently had been gleaned through the chemical analyses in which reverse engineering had been attempted. If such is the case, reverse engineering would not, and did not, constitute a misappropriation of trade secrets. In any event, it also should be noted that the new firm's products' formulations were not identical to those claimed as trade secrets by Wright. Also, as was mentioned previously, attempts to reverse engineer trade secrets from legitimately purchased products is allowable under trade secrets law. In cases in which reverse engineering can reveal one's trade secrets, trade secrets no longer exist and, therefore, do not garner the protection that the UTSA offers.

The court also found that Wright failed to prove that the former employees had utilized its confidential pricing information in their new employment. Specifically, they were charged with utilizing pricing information that had been communicated to them while they were employees of Wright through their access to the firm's fact book. The pricing and other relevant information contained in the fact book were the beneficiaries of attempts to retain confidentiality. Pages of the book clearly were marked as containing information that was confidential and not for disclosure. However, no proof was presented that the three had misappropriated such knowledge in their positions.

In short, Wright Chemical possessed trade secrets in the form of certain chemical formulations and pricing and other proprietary information. Reasonable steps had been taken to assure and maintain their secrecy, and, therefore, they were eligible for protection under the UTSA. However, Wright fell short in its attempt to prove that its former employees had misappropriated its secrets. As one might rightly conclude, Wright failed in its attempt to gain the injunction it sought.

Despite their widespread proliferation, it is a reality that microcomputers have not been around all that long. In fact, they are not much older than the UTSA itself. As is true with many new developments, the various facets related to the legality of actions surrounding the new technology raise questions that beg to be answered. Because the technologies related to microcomputer hardware and software were opening new vistas of opportunities for those engaged in their pursuit and opening new legal quandaries for those whose careers hinged on their adequate protection and security, it is not surprising that the question of trade secrets and their impact on the technology has arisen on more than one occasion.

Vault Corporation v. Quaid Software Limited is a case in point. Vault Corporation is engaged in the development and marketing of computer software technologies aimed at providing security for third-party software products. Quaid Software is a technology firm that markets a variety of software products, one of which caused Vault to bring action against Quaid, seeking an injunction to prevent it from selling the software product. Vault claimed a variety of transgressions by Quaid's product, but they hinged on charges of copyright infringement, violations of Louisiana's Software License Enforcement Act (SLEA), and, more to the purpose of the discussion at hand, violation of the firm's trade secrets under the UTSA.

Vault's product of concern in this effort can be described as a computer program imbedded on diskettes that prevents the unauthorized copying of any second-party software also residing on the diskettes. One should note that unauthorized copying of microcomputer software is a major problem for software firms and potentially has cost the industry billions of dollars. Vault's trademarked product, PROLOK, was marketed to software firms as a means of preventing unauthorized copying of their products and was seen as a potential solution to the problem. Diskettes sold by Vault containing the PROLOK protection program, on which second-party applications software would eventually reside, ostensibly would prevent individuals from making unauthorized copies of the software and selling or otherwise distributing unlicensed copies of the applications software.

Quaid, a Canadian firm, sells a variety of technology-based products, at least one of which (CopyWrite) had the ability to "unlock" the protection program-product marketed by Vault. CopyWrite would allow its user to copy programs from the protected diskettes to other diskettes or to a computer's hard disk. Quaid reported that its research and development efforts that led to the creation of CopyWrite took place at its Canadian offices after Quaid legitimately acquired copies of PROLOK software by mail. Although CopyWrite was capable of unlocking PROLOK and allowing copies to be made of software so protected, it had various other diagnostic and copying capabilities for which it also was in demand. Quaid marketed its products to U.S. customers, primarily through mail order. Its advertisements, noting CopyWrite software was priced at $50, were placed primarily in major microcomputer magazines.

The CopyWrite software was said to allow users to make legitimate archival copies of their software. A backup copy of software often is desired by those whose time and energies are spent in computer environments. Should an original software product that cannot be copied get destroyed or otherwise become unusable, the individual who depends on the product to conduct business would be placed in a situation of being unable to recover in a timely manner and, as a result, find that work can no longer proceed as usual but, instead, is delayed while a replacement copy of the needed software is secured. Thus, the ability to make and secure copies of vital computer software often is seen as a necessity by those who desire not to be subject to the vagaries of computer life, in which everything hinges on the viability of only one diskette.

Quaid's expectation that its product would be used only for making legitimate backup copies of software was reflected in its advertising copy. A statement was included in its instruction manuals accompanying its product that reinforced the notion that only legitimate backup copies of software be created and that the software should not be used to create illegal copies of any copyrighted software. Further, Quaid reported that its software incorporated a "coding" provision that could allow the tracing of any copies of programs back to the original diskette and that it was taking steps to prosecute persons found guilty of using its product to make illegal copies of software.

Vault sought an injunction that would prevent Quaid from selling CopyWrite software with the capability of unlocking its PROLOK software product and the confiscation of any CopyWrite software with the unlocking capability. Vault's actions were predicated on its claims that Quaid had breached Vault's licensing agreement, that it misappropriated its trade secret, and that Quaid was infringing or contributorily infringing on its copyright on PROLOK software.

As is noted elsewhere in this book, the court will consider four factors in deciding whether an injunction will ensue: the existence of a substantial likelihood that the plaintiff would prevail on the merits of the case presented, whether the plaintiff will suffer irreparable harm if injunctive relief is denied, whether the threatened harm to the plaintiff outweighs the threatened harm to the defendant if an injunction ensues, and whether an injunction would best serve the public interest. The trial court must consider each of these factors when deciding whether or not to issue an injunction. A negative finding on any one of the four factors will preclude the court from issuing the injunction.

The court first took up the question of copyright infringement and its related charge of contributorily aiding infringement of copyright. It found that no significant similarity existed between CopyWrite and PROLOK and that any copying that had occurred years previously was not significant. It also found that the part of the CopyWrite program that allowed the unlocking of PROLOK software did not constitute a derivative work of the latter. On the charge of contributorily infringing on copyrights of software protected by PROLOK, the court took the position that Vault was not the proper claimant to pursue such a charge. Only companies whose software products are being infringed can pursue such an action. In other words, Vault was deemed to not be in the legal position of making a charge that some other firms' software products were being infringed. If the rights of others are being infringed, then those whose rights are being infringed need to make such a charge should they deem it necessary. Despite the ruling that Vault was not the correct party to file a contributory infringement action, the court, nevertheless, noted that it could find no contributory infringement in the evidence presented. The ability of CopyWrite to make legitimate archival copies of software met the "archival exception" as embodied in copyright law. The archival exception gives legitimate computer software owners the right to make archival copies of their legally purchased software delivered via a medium that may be subject to destruction or damage. Congress obviously felt it important that legitimate users of computer software not be placed in a position of violating federal law by merely providing for the continuation of their computer utilization should a catastrophic occurrence impact the usability of their software. The court found that CopyWrite as developed and marketed was capable of being utilized for "commercially significant noninfringing uses" and, therefore, did not infringe on Vault's copyright.

In deliberating as to the potential violation of the UTSA as adopted by Louisiana, the court considered closely the definitions contained within the act. One of Vault's claims centered on its contention that Quaid's research and development efforts, which included the decompiling and disassembling of a copy of PROLOK, amounted to a violation of its trade secrets. Specifically, Vault claimed that Quaid's actions violated its trade secrets, because a licensing agreement present on packages of PROLOK software prohibited the decompiling or disassembly of

PROLOK software without the prior written permission of Vault Corporation.

The UTSA stipulates that a trade secret comprises information, including a formula, pattern, compilation, program, device, method, technique, or process, that derives independent economic value from not being generally known to and not being readily ascertainable by proper means by other persons who can obtain economic value from its disclosure or use and is subject to efforts that are reasonable under the circumstances to maintain its secrecy. On the surface, one may conclude that computer programs always are protected as trade secrets because they are included specifically in the definition of a trade secret. However, it would be a mistake to separate the word "program" from the context of the remainder of the definition. The definition stipulates that the information be in such a state as to not be readily ascertainable through proper means by other persons. If a computer program is ascertainable by proper means or if the program is not the subject of efforts that are reasonable under the circumstances to maintain its secrecy, then it does not meet the definition of a trade secret and, therefore, would not be eligible for protection under the UTSA.

The PROLOK software was proprietary information that possessed independent economic value. Vault Corporation had taken steps that were construed to be reasonable in their ability to maintain the secrecy of the program. Among the security provisions pursued to maintain secrecy were provisions for encrypting the software code in four layers, separating the programmers who worked on the various layers from one another, having employees sign nondisclosure agreements, using shredding devices to destroy surplus paper copies of the program, storing the master copy of the program in a locked safe, including explicit licensing agreements on the product, and periodically changing the product's code to make disassembly more difficult. So, PROLOK had economic value and was subject to efforts that were deemed reasonable under the circumstances to maintain its secrecy. However, the question that is germane to the discussion is whether or not the information was readily ascertainable through proper means by persons who could obtain economic benefit from its use or disclosure.

In this case, there was no question that PROLOK had been decompiled and disassembled by Quaid. Quaid purchased the software through legitimate sources in the open market. So, does the act of decompiling and disassembling the PROLOK code give rise to an act of trade secrets misappropriation? It does not give rise to a misappropriation under the auspices of the UTSA. Decompiling and disassembling a software code is a technological form of reverse engineering, which, as seen under *Acuson v. Aloka*, essentially can be a legal exercise under the provisions of the UTSA. Note that there can be no secret inherent in information that can be learned through proper means, and reverse engineering normally is viewed as using proper means when the item in question has been obtained on the open market in a legal manner. Still, there is the question as to whether the reverse engineering in this case was proper, given the license agreement on the package that prohibited such acts.

Vault claimed that Quaid's actions were tantamount to violations of the Louisiana SLEA and the UTSA. Therein lies a question on which much hinges. Louisiana law considers the type of license agreement found on a package of software to be an "adhesion" contract. An adhesion contract is a contract that is drafted unilaterally by the seller and presented on a take-it-or-leave-it basis to the buyer. Much software being sold today is accompanied by such licensing, which typically states that, by opening the package or breaking the seal, the buyer is agreeing to the terms of the license (contract). In the case of Vault's software, the license contains a choice of law provision that stipulates to the purchaser that, to the extent that the laws of the United States are found not applicable to the terms and conditions of the license, the license shall be governed by the laws of the state of Louisiana. A choice of law provision designates which state's laws will govern the terms of the agreement to the extent that its law does not preempt or is contrary to federal law. In cases in which a specific state is designated in a choice of law contract, it generally is accepted that the state law will not, or cannot, deny benefits allowable under federal law or otherwise overstep explicit federal legislation.

The court had to determine whether Louisiana law contained stipulations that were contrary to the Copyright Act or otherwise stood to be preempted by its specific provisions. In short, the Louisiana's SLEA allows a purchaser to be bound by the provisions of a contract of adhesion. Such contracts were expected to be statutorily binding to the purchaser when they contained prohibitions against a variety of specific unauthorized activities, including code translations, decompilations, disassemblings, and reverse engineering. However, the court found that specific provisions that prohibited copying for any purpose were in direct violation of copyright law, which allows for the copying of software for archival purposes and other reasons deemed essential to utilize a computer program. Additional provisions of the SLEA were seen as contrary to the Copyright Act. Vault's case, though, was not preempted by the Copyright Act. As the court noted, patent and copyright protection are effective in providing for the protection of products so registered. However, trade secrets law is less effective than the federal statutes in providing protection and, therefore, is not preempted by specific federal law.

One of the major shortcomings of trade secrets law is the realization that it does not protect against discovery and use through independent invention, accidental or willful disclosure, or reverse-engineering efforts. The court noted that provisions of Louisiana's SLEA contravened provisions of the Copyright Act. Specifically, the SLEA prohibits any copying of software products while the Copyright Act allows archival copying, and the SLEA extends such exclusivity into perpetuity as opposed to the Copyright Act's provision of 50 years beyond the life of the author. As a result, the court found certain provisions of the PROLOK licensing agreement to be unenforceable to the extent that they violated the Copyright Act. As a consequence of the license agreement being unenforceable, its prohibitions against reverse engineering (decompiling and translating) could not stand. The result was that Vault could not prove adequately that Quaid had violated its trade secrets, nor did it prove to the satisfaction of the court that the action resulted in an unlawful misappropriation. The request for an injunction prohibiting the sale of CopyWrite software capable of unlocking PROLOK was denied.

If one's atmosphere of confidentiality is so lax as to allow outsiders ready access to the trade secret, then the protectable nature of the secret no longer exists. The atmosphere of confidentiality must be at the heart of all efforts to maintain secrecy and must permeate the firm's secrecy efforts. When one knowingly reveals one's secrets or is so lax as to allow others to view or learn the secret, then the UTSA will not protect the information as a secret. The UTSA offers its protection for the protection of trade secrets. If information is not secret or becomes widely known, it no longer enjoys the benefits offered by trade secrets law.

In *Sheets v. Yamaha Motors Corporation, U.S.A.*, it was seen that willfully permitting others to see and photograph an item may remove any protection that is sought under the UTSA. In this case, the purported inventor of a snorkel device and tuning process for air intake systems for tri-motorcycles sought damages against Yamaha in part under Louisiana's version of the UTSA. The specifics of the case history indicated that the plaintiff's sons publicly raced tri-motorcycles that incorporated Sheet's modifications. His sons' motorcycle dealership reportedly made similar modifications on motorcycles for friends and motorcycles belonging to other members of their racing team. Motorcycles belonging to Sheet's sons and others to which the modifications had been made became widely known in racing circles for their ability to traverse relatively wet environments without faltering. This ability to traverse deep water apparently gave the riders an edge in cross-country races that included water crossings as a part of the race trial.

It was reported that, after Sheets' sons became known for their deep water racing successes, Yamaha representatives visited the Sheets' dealership and photographed the snorkel device. At the request of Yamaha, Sheets allowed a tri-motorcycle with his device attached to be exhibited before a meeting of Yamaha employees and dealers. About a year later, Sheets noticed an advertisement for Yamaha's new line of 175 tri-motorcycles with air intake system modifications similar to those he had purportedly pioneered.

Sheets filed suit against Yamaha, alleging misappropriation of trade secrets. He subsequently applied for a patent on the device, but the application was rejected, ostensibly because Yamaha previously had been granted patents on essentially the same device. The district court dismissed the case after finding that Sheets failed to maintain the secrecy of his invention and, thus, could not recover damages under Louisiana's UTSA. The appeals court agreed, noting that Sheets failed to maintain the secrecy of the device, had willingly displayed it to Yamaha representatives and others, had willingly allowed it to be photographed, had installed the device and made the necessary modifications on several tri-motorcycles belonging to various individuals, and had given only minimal instructions to those whose motorcycles had received the modification as to the necessity of not revealing the modification to others. In short, there was no atmosphere of confidentiality, and it did not appear that reasonable efforts were expended to maintain the secrecy of the information. The primary necessity for developing and maintaining an atmosphere of confidentiality lies at the heart of trade secrets protection. Reasonable efforts to protect one's trade secrets must be made in order to garner the protection that many seek.

In still another case in which secrecy or lack thereof weighed heavily on the court's decision, Rockwell Graphic System, Incorporated, failed in its attempt to protect what it viewed as its proprietary property. In *Rockwell Graphic System, Inc. v. Dev Industries et al.*, the district court upheld the lower court ruling that Rockwell Graphic System's treatment of its piece part drawings was not sufficiently protective to establish their secrecy under Illinois trade secret law. In Illinois, as in many jurisdictions, the question of secrecy is relative. The disclosure of secret information to a customer or others on a need to know basis for business purposes does not, in all cases, destroy the confidentiality or secrecy of information involved. However, there is an expectation of the courts that secrecy will be maintained both within a business and without. There is an explicit expectation that disclosure of trade secret information will be limited to those with a need to know and that a reasonable effort will be made to maintain the secrecy of trade secrets.

Rockwell Graphic System is engaged in the manufacture, installation, and maintenance of printing equipment. It was noted that, as a part of its design and manufacturing efforts, the firm had produced over 1 million piece part drawings since it had begun operations. Rockwell's assertion that its trade secrets had been misappropriated referred to the misappropriation of a group of specific drawings the firm considered trade secrets. Despite having over 1 million piece part drawings, the firm did not consider all of its drawings as being trade secrets. The drawings in question were viewed as trade secrets by the firm's management, and this case was pursued on the basis of the belief that the firm's secrets had been misappropriated.

Rockwell admitted providing assembly piece part drawings to the *Chicago Tribune* to ease the newspaper publisher's efforts at maintaining printing equipment it had purchased from Rockwell. Several other major newspaper publishers apparently had been supplied with various assembly drawings for similar purposes. Although the detailed drawings had statements to the effect that the drawings were the property of MGD Graphic Systems (a division of Rockwell) and were "loaned in confidence subject to return upon request," included the provision that "no copies could be made without the written consent of MGD Graphic Systems," and had statements that all rights to the design or invention were reserved, Rockwell did not contend that the drawings given to these customers were trade secrets.

Further, it was reported that Rockwell did not attempt to control the duplication of the drawings and did not keep an inventory of or track those drawings that had been loaned out. In addition, it appeared that Rockwell had never insisted that any of its piece part drawings be returned.

Although these drawings were not considered to be trade secrets by Rockwell, in many instances, they contained sufficient ancillary material to allow for the production of the parts detailed in the drawings. Specific dimensions, tolerances, finishes, and additional information that would ease the manufacturing of the parts by those in possession of the drawings were included on the diagrams provided.

At the time of the district court proceedings, Dev had been engaged in manufacturing printing press parts for over a decade. Early in its existence, the firm had hired two former employees of Rockwell Graphic System and, as a result, came into possession of approximately 100 of the piece part drawings produced by Rockwell. For some time, Dev duplicated various Rockwell parts using the drawings. This part manufacturing effort was without Rockwell's knowledge or consent.

Several of Rockwell's employees gave similar statements concerning the firm's piece part drawings and the procedures surrounding their use and disposition. In general, their statements described the firm's position with regard to the drawings as one of concern. Employee statements attested to the notion that Rockwell made efforts to limit the information provided in the drawings to the minimal amount necessary for a vendor-manufacturer to adequately manufacture replacement parts for older equipment (ostensibly with Rockwell's permission). The information also was seen as being necessary to provide complimentary equipment manufacturers with the ability to better interface their auxiliary items or equipment with that of Rockwell's installations. All drawings loaned to these vendors were stamped "confidential" and included statements on expectations of confidentiality and rights reservations, as already mentioned. Employees felt that the lending of piece part drawings to customers was a rare occurrence.

Rockwell's customer service department had its own internal security procedures regarding the drawings. Employees desiring drawings had to sign them out as a part of this standard procedure. On completing the task for which the piece part drawing was needed, employees were expected to dispose of the copies. Early on, discarded copies simply had been thrown out in the trash, but for quite some time, the firm's expectation included the provision that employees should shred piece part drawings and similar documents to prevent their disclosure or unauthorized dissemination.

Testimony from customers and employees was inconsistent. Customers noted that they were in possession of many drawings, some of which had been obtained from Rockwell and some from other firms in the industry. It was revealed that an active "user group" of firms using Rockwell's equipment was in existence. The group's members regularly swapped piece part drawings. One firm reportedly had in its possession several boxes of Rockwell's piece part drawings. Another firm supposedly had a number of piece part drawings in addition to those needed to maintain its own equipment.

Rockwell's complaint centered on a group of 100 piece part drawings that Dev had obtained from two of Rockwell's former employees. Even though Rockwell did not consider all of its drawings to comprise trade secret information, it did consider the 100 piece part drawings in the possession of Dev as its proprietary property. Despite Rockwell's arguments, the courts found that the drawings in Dev's possession were not trade secrets deserving protection under the law. The evidence presented did not indicate that the parts in question were treated any differently than the myriad of other drawings in the possession of numerous customers and equipment manufacturers, nor, apparently, was their release considered such a rare occurrence.

The court noted that Rockwell had failed to take reasonable security precautions to protect its piece part drawings from disclosure to competitors who might use them to Rockwell's disadvantage. Indeed, even in its own internal operations, despite having to sign out drawings, employees were not monitored to assure that discarded drawings were shredded, an inventory of drawings was not adequately maintained, no one could account for the number or location of copies outstanding, and there was no evidence presented that would indicate that Rockwell's own employees were under a restrictive covenant not to disclose the information to third parties. Plant security was described as being no greater than one would expect in any commercial facility aimed at protecting the facility from outside intruders. Given that the atmosphere of confidentiality at Rockwell relative to its piece part drawings appeared insufficient to protect valuable trade secrets, it is not surprising that the court found the drawings in Dev's possession not to be secret and, therefore, ineligible for protection under trade secrets law.

Several cases have centered around the question of customer lists and the appropriateness of their continued use by former employees while working for new employers. This is especially critical in situations in which the customer lists are considered to be trade secrets of a firm. There appears to be no question that a firm can require new recruits to sign confidentiality agreements that forbid the use of customer lists construed to be secrets as a requisite for hiring. The promise of employment and the signing are seen as providing legal consideration, making such a contract enforceable. However, the question that begs to be answered is whether a firm can enforce a confidentiality agreement signed by an individual who already is employed by the firm. In other words, is there sufficient legal consideration given on the part of the firm that would allow it to enforce confidentiality agreements imposed on existing employees? A case arose that addressed this question and shed light on an area that is of concern to many firms that are just beginning to recognize their need to develop an atmosphere of confidentiality in their work environment.

Insurance Associates Corporation v. Hansen et al., is a case that lends credence to the use of confidentiality agreements with existing employees. In this case, Hansen was a former agent of Insurance Associates who had worked for the firm for approximately two years prior to entering into a written employment agreement with the firm. The agreement acknowledged that Hansen would not solicit business from any customers of Insurance Associates with whom Hansen had conducted business or personal affairs during the term of the written agreement for a period of two years following termination of his employment at Insurance Associates. The agreement also stated that written consent of Insurance Associates was necessary to use the firm's confidential information, including information relating to customers or accounts of Insurance Associates, encompassing the names of the customers, policy terms, conditions, rates, customer risk profiles, and information concerning the market for large or unusual risks as handled by Insurance Associates. Further, a statement in the agreement stipulated that all records, files, manuals, lists of customers, blanks, forms, materials, supplies, and computer programs entrusted to Hansen by Insurance Associates belonged to the firm and would be surrendered to the firm upon the termination of Hansen's employment.

Hansen continued to be employed by Insurance Associates for a period of approximately eight months after signing the agreement. Reportedly, he then was fired and, in less than two weeks, had begun working at Swan Insurance Agency, a codefendant in this case. Over 20 of Hansen's former customers at Insurance Associates quickly moved their coverage to Hansen at his new place of employment. Insurance Associates sued Hansen and the Swan Agency, claiming violation of the employment agreement's strict prohibition against the solicitation, directly or indirectly, of business from any Insurance Associates customer with whom Hansen had conducted business or with whom he had personal relationships during his employment. Among remedies desired, Insurance Associates sought damages for lost commissions pursuant to a clause in the agreement that stated that all premiums, commissions, or fees collected from customers belonged to Insurance Associates.

Hansen's arguments to the contrary covered several legal questions, but the one of current concern was the argument that proffered that Insurance Associates had not given sufficient consideration on which to base a legally enforceable contract. In essence, Hansen argued that, because he already was employed by Insurance Associates, he had not received consideration for his signing of the contract, a factor he claimed would make the agreement unenforceable.

In contract law, consideration is required of both entities to a contract. The idea behind consideration in a contractual arrangement is that each party brings something to the table. Entering a contract requires that both parties give something or give up something in order for the terms of the agreement to be viewed as enforceable. Hansen indicated that, because he already was employed by Insurance Associates, the firm had not given him anything (consideration) in order to get him to sign the contract, and because he had not received anything from the firm, the specifics of the agreement were unenforceable.

Following the lead of the district court, the court of appeals failed to concur with Hansen's arguments concerning lack of consideration on the part of Insurance Associates. The court noted that Hansen continued to be employed for eight months following the signing of the employment agreement. If Hansen had not signed the agreement, his employment would have been terminated. Thus, the promise of continued employment by Insurance Associates was sufficient consideration to bind Hansen to the agreement.

As the Commissioners on Uniform State Laws proffer in their notes accompanying the UTSA, the public disclosure of trade secret information, even through carelessness, can preclude protection of the information through the UTSA. In *Secure Services Technology, Inc., v. Time and Space Processing, Inc.*, the plaintiff failed to gain protection of its "handshake protocol" used in the transmission of classified information when the court found that insufficient steps had been taken to insure the confidentiality of the information. It was noted that Secure Services Technology had failed to take advantage of federal law that allows vendors of goods to the military to be granted protection of proprietary information by merely noting such on their vouchers. The plaintiff's failure to adequately maintain a climate of confidentiality (that is, failing to delineate the secrecy of the protocol and the absence of a declaration retaining the rights to the protocol) gave the government unlimited rights to the protocol, effectively putting the protocol in the public domain and waiving any trade secret protection that might have arisen under the UTSA.

The Freedom of Information Act (FoIA) is a federal law that allows access to unclassified government information by the members of the general public. Although an in-depth discussion of the FoIA and its impact on business executives and their competitive efforts is beyond the scope of this discussion, the intent of the law, the types of information it exempts from its reporting requirements, its relationship to trade secrets law, and its impact on confidentiality need to be recognized by executives who are responsible for implementing trade secrets protection strategies. A brief overview of the FoIA provides executives with insight into the risks to trade secrets that exist in its implementation.

In providing information to federal agencies as directed by statutorily imposed reporting requirements, one does expose one's trade secrets to potential disclosure. Still, in those cases in which the reporting of information that may be construed to be among a firm's trade secrets is required by federal statute or agency regulations, executives need to do so with an effort to providing for continuous protection of such secrets.

The FoIA was enacted in 1966 with the purpose of providing for an informed public who, being so informed, can better participate in government scrutiny efforts and be in a better position to contribute to the democratic process. The "openness" that the FoIA fosters is, arguably, an admirable goal. Indeed, as a reaffirmation of the act's original intent, President Bill Clinton in October 1993 requested that federal agencies renew their commitment to the expectation of government openness embodied within the act. The act requires that information in the possession of federal agencies will be made available to those requesting such access through appropriate channels. The good news for those who must reveal trade secrets to governmental agencies, as may be required through a governmental information collection process, is that the FoIA specifically exempts nine categories of information from public disclosure. Information meeting criteria that delineate that information as one of these nine categories can and will be withheld from public disclosure. Employees of agencies who are requested to provide information found in any of these nine categories are not expected to release such information.

The first exemption protects information that is deemed to be in the interest of providing or maintaining the nation's security. This exemption applies to information concerning the national defense, the release of which may imperil the safety of the country. The same exemption applies to information of a foreign policy nature that might compromise the security of the nation. It is expected that information not released pursuant to the first exemption will have been appropriately classified in accordance with procedures as contained in executive orders concerning classified information.

The FoIA recognizes that agency personnel rules and practices are exempt from public disclosure. For those matters deemed to be related solely to internal personnel rules and practices, mandatory disclosure of the information is exempted. This exemption appears to be predicated on the basis of the trivial nature of such matters and the nonexistent public interest in such matters, especially in light of their not possessing substance of a significant or genuine interest. In essence, agencies are not expected to gather and supply information on each and every potential agency personnel rule that it may impose on its employees or use in the personnel process when there is no reasonable expectation that a real public interest could be served by the release of such information.

The third exemption allows that information will not be disclosed when such a prohibition is specifically embodied in another federal statute. An amendment to the act in 1976 specifies that statutorily imposed prohibitions must meet one of two conditions in order for information to qualify under exemption three of the act. To qualify, a statute's language must be specific in its delineation of information prohibited from disclosure and leave no room for discretion on the part of the agency to deliberate its disposition or establish explicit criteria, the meeting of which establishes exemption or is specific as to which types of information are to be withheld. Given that an information item meets one of these conditions, it is exempted from disclosure under the FoIA.

Exemption four of the FoIA is the major one of concern to those responsible for the protection of trade secrets. The fourth exemption explicitly prohibits the public disclosure of trade secrets and commercial or financial information that is privileged or confidential. This exemption recognizes that the disclosure of confidential information or trade secrets as required by agencies pursuant to federal statutes poses a risk to the competitive situation of firms and, therefore, the information deserves protection from disclosure. A determination by a federal agency that specific information falls within the context of exemption four is tantamount to a decision that the information cannot be released.

Three points are worth noting here. First, the definition of a trade secret in the context of federal law does not conform exactly with the definition of trade secrets under the UTSA; there are differences. Second, even though there is a prohibition against the public release of such information, inadvertent leaks may occur. Finally, these two concerns again emphasize the importance of seeking competent legal counsel when the release of trade secrets information is being considered pursuant to some court order or federal statute requirement.

Exemption five specifies that documents arising from interagency or intraagency memos or letters would not be available by law to another who is involved in litigation with the agency. Specifically, this exemption prohibits from disclosure those documents germane to a litigation that normally would be construed to be privileged information.

The sixth exemption prohibits the release of information about individuals contained in personnel files, medical files, and other clearly similar files where the release of such information would constitute an invasion of an individual's privacy. An exception to exemption six does allow an individual to request such private information that is contained in such files and concerns themselves. Obviously, persons obtaining information about their own personnel files, for instance, would not be invading their own privacy.

Records of law enforcement agencies compiled for law enforcement purposes generally are exempt from disclosure. There are several categories of law enforcement information covered under exemption seven of the act. Information that would reveal the identities of confidential informants, deprive an individual of a fair trial, or imperil the life or safety of an individual and a variety of other information in the possession of law enforcement agencies, the disclosure of which may imperil enforcement actions to an extent as to allow the circumvention of the law, are exempt from disclosure.

Exemption eight under the FoIA covers information that was obtained as a result of an examination or reports prepared by or on behalf of an agency responsible for the regulation or supervision of financial institutions. Based on court decisions, it appears that the term "financial institutions" does not refer just to banks, savings and loans, and credit unions but also to other regulated institutions that can be construed to be financial institutions, including stock exchanges.

The last exemption prohibits the release of certain information as it relates to wells and related geological exploratory activities. Specifically, exemption nine prohibits the release of geological or geophysical information, data, maps, and related information concerning wells.

The FoIA stipulates that information in the possession of federal agencies will be accessible by members of the public. That is the bad news. The good news is that exemption four precludes the release of information that is considered a trade secret or commercial information that is confidential and privileged. However, it is important to recognize that government agencies to whom trade secrets have been delivered must be made aware of the presence of the secrets in order to effect adequate measures to maintain such secrets and to minimize their inadvertent disclosure in response to requests filed under the FoIA or similar right to know legislation.

It would be nice if the word "minimize" in the preceding sentence was the word "prevent." However, this is not a perfect world. People in the employ of the federal government are expected to enforce the provisions of the FoIA, including its exemptions. A problem facing those who are responsible for trade secrets protection is the realization that people make mistakes, and, therefore, sometimes prohibited disclosures occur. In his article "The Costs of Free Information," Richard A. Guida (1989) relates a news story detailing how the Environmental Protection Agency (EPA) mistakenly released the formula for a Monsanto Corporation herbicide, which caused that firm to lose its dominant market position in what was then a $450 million annual market. More recently, David Hanson (1994) reports that a suit has been filed against the EPA, charging it with violations of the FoIA and the Administrative Procedures Act. The suit specifically seeks information concerning inert ingredients used in pesticides, which chemical firms claim to be confidential information and which the EPA refuses to release.

The serious threat to trade secrets potentially at risk under the FoIA goes beyond the occasional error on the part of an employee. The originator of information being submitted to an agency must be careful to strongly emphasize and indicate to the agency the presence in a report of information construed to be trade secrets. It is imperative that the owners of trade secrets be proactive in their pronouncements and delineations of trade secrets contained in agency reports. Too, it is important that submitters of such reports realize that they are better off submitting that which is required but to remain vigilant in submissions to agencies in order to preclude other, nonrequested secrets from being divulged.

Undoubtedly, the FoIA has been a boon to those seeking information on the activities of government agencies. However, it has serious drawbacks that imperil the rights of others. It is not by chance that the majority of requests being filed under the auspices of the FoIA are being filed by businesses seeking information on competitors, and perhaps not surprisingly, the second largest number of filings of FoIA requests are being filed by prisoners and other crime figures seeking information that may prove of worth to them. Guida (1989) cites Food & Drug Administration officials as stating that 80 percent of their FoIA requests in one year were filings by commercial firms. Clearly, the risk of public disclosure of trade secrets through governmental filings exists. It is important that executives remain vigilant in all of their efforts and provide for the continued maintenance of secrecy with regard to their trade secrets.

Despite the provision for exemptions, the government agency retains the authority to withhold or release requested information. It is up to the firm to make the case to the federal agency that the information in question is a trade secret and that it must be protected. If an agency disagrees as to the proprietary nature of information submitted, a firm may find that its only recourse is to file a federal suit to prevent the disclosure. One's legal counsel is in the best position to advise on this matter.

For one desiring detailed information on the FoIA, assistance is available from the U.S. Government Printing Office in Washington, D.C. The *Freedom of Information Act Guide & Privacy Act Overview* (1994) is a 600-page treatise detailing the acts and their implications. Although it is the legal sourcebook on the two acts and provides much information, its reading is not for the faint of heart; still, its reading is encouraged.

There have been multiple cases in which determinations had to be made as to whether an entity was a government agency or a private firm. In such a case, the question arose as to whether an organization was, in fact, a government entity and, thus, subject to that state's public records act (PRA), which has a purpose parallel to that of the FoIA. The PRA intends that full and complete disclosure relative to the affairs of government shall be forthcoming and easily obtained by those outside the bounds of government. The case, *Indianapolis Convention & Visitors Association, Inc., v. Indianapolis Newspapers, Inc.* was anxiously watched by many involved in quasi-governmental bodies, because its impact went far beyond the confines of Indianapolis. In this case, the Indianapolis Convention and Visitors Association was requested by the newspaper to provide the newspaper with various financial information relative to the association's operations. The Convention Association declined to provide the requested information, contending that it was not a state agency subject to the PRA. The Convention Association asserted that it was a private association and, thus, outside the scope of the PRA, that some of the information requested fell into the category of trade secrets, and that revealing the information would put the association in a weakened competitive position, because competitors could, potentially, request its secrets.

Complicating the case somewhat at the time it was filed was the fact that some of the association's financial support came from its 600-plus members and some of its support came from a distribution of collected tax monies. The public tax monies came into the Convention Association via the Capital Improvement Board, itself a government entity supported with the proceeds of the area's hotel and motel occupancy tax. The Capital Improvement Board funded promotional efforts initiated by both governmental and private groups whose efforts were focused on promoting tourism in the area, especially in the vicinity of the convention center. Further, Indiana law construes liberally the meaning of public agency and includes those entities receiving support in the form of public distributions that are not considered direct payments for goods or services acquired through state or municipal procurement.

The Indiana Supreme Court ruled that the association was, in fact, subject to the PRA, because monies received were not always identifiable with specific purchases of products or services from the association. It was noted that the association's income tax returns categorized funding from the Capital Improvement Board as "indirect public support," not as earned income from providing a service to the board. Also, a preamble to an agreement between the board and the association mentioned that the board financially supported the association, partly through the provision of free office space, furniture, and equipment. Finally, the association was subject to audit by the state board of accounts, which is responsible for auditing agencies or entities that are maintained or supported in whole or in part by public funds. As a result, the supreme court found that the association was a public entity within the meaning of Indiana law and that it was subject to the provisions of the PRA.

A different case with a somewhat similar situation involved a power company that did not want its price and volume data, information it claimed to be a trade secret, made public. In *Northern States Power Company v. North Dakota Public Service Commission*, the power company sued to have its price and volume data contained in required filings with the public service commission (PSC) declared a trade secret, thus, preventing its public disclosure by the PSC. The courts agreed that price and volume data could constitute a trade secret under the UTSA but that price and volume data contained in PSC filings were not exempt from North Dakota's open records law. Essentially, the court felt that the higher need related to legitimate governmental interest in policing irregularities and handling public matters affecting rates for essential commodities, including those products handled by the public utilities of the state, meant that the power company could have no reasonable expectation that its price and volume data would be restricted from scrutiny and public inspection.

There was still another instance in which government disclosure statutes were seen as providing a state with a legitimate right to know in order to monitor compliance with state law. Again, the state's right to know was shown to supersede a firm's expectation or desire that it be precluded from revealing what it considered to be confidential information as provided in the UTSA. In the case of *State of Alaska, Department of Natural Resources v. Artic Slope Regional Corporation et al.*, oil companies had claimed that their well data comprised some of their trade secrets and that a requirement by the Department of Natural Resources that they provide such information to the state amounted to an illegal taking of private property.

It was noted that, in Alaska, state law requires oil drilling firms operating within the state on leased lands to provide substantial well data to the state. The statute allows for a two-year confidentiality period, during which the information is not released to the public. At the end of the two years, a firm may file for an extension of the confidentiality period if it deems prudent.

In this case, the drilling firms did not apply for an extension. Instead, they sued the state's Department of Natural Resources, claiming, among other things, that its reporting requirements infringed on their trade secrets and that the reporting requirement and the subsequent disclosure of the information at the end of the two year period was an illegal taking of their property. The court found that the information was valuable and secret and that the firms exerted reasonable efforts to keep the information confidential. In short, the information was a trade secret.

The superior court found for the oil firms, noting that the information was a trade secret and that making the information public at the end of the confidentiality period amounted to an unconstitutional taking of property. Although the supreme court of Alaska also found the information to be trade secrets and protectable under the law, it reversed the superior court's injunction, noting that the public reporting of the well data without provision for compensating the oil firms for their property did not amount to an unconstitutional taking of property. It was noted that the Department of Natural Resource's lawful charge over the state's resources has at its core the expectation that such resources will be managed in a manner so as to achieve the maximum benefit for the people of the state. The right to know expectation is paramount under the legislature's directive, given the department's charge. Therefore, the information reporting did not amount to an unconstitutional taking of property.

What about a situation in which both copyright infringement and trade secrets misappropriation are alleged? Can a trade secret exist in a situation in which another has the right to make public the information that comprises the secret?

As mentioned earlier, there are times when federal laws do not preempt actions filed under state law. Under Virginia's trade secrets statute, it can be seen that recovery from trade secret misappropriation requires proof of breach of confidence beyond that which would be necessary to recover in an action for copyright infringement.

In *Avtec Systems Incorporated v. Peiffer et al.*, questions relating to copyright infringement and trade secret misappropriation converged. The background of the case revealed that Peiffer developed a software program during the time of his employ at Avtec. Questions arose as to whether subsequent versions of the program were produced "for hire" or were completed on Peiffer's personal time for his own purposes. It was proffered that, after the first version of the program was demonstrated to customers, Avtec announced a new policy, a written announcement binding employees to duties of confidentiality and nondisclosure respecting the firm's proprietary and trade secrets — a policy of which Peiffer was supposedly aware.

After demonstrating the original version of the software, Peiffer made changes in the program, based on bugs found by Avtec employees. Later, Peiffer sold the exclusive rights of the updated, corrected program to a competitive firm. Avtec moved to copyright the original version of the program and filed suit, charging copyright infringement and misappropriation of trade secrets, among other claims. Shortly thereafter, Peiffer filed copyright registration on both the original version and an expanded, updated version of the program. The defendants then counterclaimed for copyright infringement by Avtec.

The appeals court remanded the question of copyright infringement back to the district court. On the question of trade secrets misappropriation, the court focused its deliberations on two major concerns.

First, the defendants argued that the trade secrets claim is preempted by the copyright infringement action. The preemption defense was rejected on the basis that recovery for trade secret misappropriation requires proof of breach of confidence — an element of proof beyond that which is necessary for recovery in an action brought for copyright infringement. Because the copyright ownership of the original program had not been established clearly by the district court, that part of the case was remanded to the district court for further consideration. However, the notion that copyright law would preempt trade secrets law in the trade secrets arena was quickly laid to rest.

Second, the defendant argued that the trade secrets claim should fail on its merits, because he owned the copyright of the program and, therefore, could not misappropriate his own work. The district court, though, held that Avtec had an interest in the program, described variously as a trade secret or as a license, relative to the use of the original program. However, the defendants questioned the judgment that based its findings on trade secrets law if, in fact, the firm did not have exclusive license to the program. As one might expect, a secret that is not a secret all of the time to all of the parties involved cannot stand as a secret. As a result, the question of state trade secrets law violation was remanded to the district court.

The appeals court noted that, should the district court find that Peiffer does own the copyright to all versions of the program and that Avtec has a nonexclusive license to use the program, then Avtec's claim of trade secret misappropriation would fail. A nonexclusive license to use a program, controlled by another who can publish it at will, does not "support the reasonable expectation of secrecy necessary to predicate a claim that the identical material is a trade secret under Virginia law." So, if Peiffer is shown to own the program and makes public use of the program by selling it to others, Avtec's claim to have secrets in the program would not stand.

It was interesting to note in this case that, although the questions of copyright ownership and trade secrets misappropriation were remanded to the district court, the finding that Peiffer breached his fiduciary duties owed to Avtec was affirmed. The court found that Peiffer breached his fiduciary duties through his nondisclosure of his relationship with the competitor and by demonstrating only the early version of the program to Avtec's customers, an act that could not be construed to be in the better interest of Avtec.

In *Lamb-Weston, Inc., v. McCain Foods, LTD.*, the plaintiff claimed that its trade secrets as embodied in a proprietary helical slicing blade used in the production of curlicue french fries had been misappropriated. The firm had a patent application pending on the blade slicing system, but the information it contained still was seen as confidential at the time of the misappropriation.

Lamb-Weston is engaged in the food processing business in Oregon. Specifically, it produces a variety of potato-based products. It had worked for several years to develop the technology that enabled the expedient production of curlicue french fries. Three years after Lamb-Weston began developing its helical bladed system, McCain, one of Lamb-Weston's competitors, also began to develop the process in earnest.

McCain purportedly solicited help from various Lamb-Weston employees. One of these employees is said to have provided McCain with a copy of the confidential patent application that was under review. Subsequently, that employee left Lamb-Weston and was in turn employed by McCain. An independent contractor who had worked on the Lamb-Weston effort for some time and who was responsible for crafting the specialized blades used in the water feed system was contracted by McCain to supply it with a helical blade capable of cutting potatoes into curlicues. McCain gave no specific instructions as to the design process nor were materials specified for use in the blade. McCain knew of the contractor's connection with Lamb-Weston.

A few months later, the patent application was approved, and Lamb-Weston was issued patents for its helical blade, water feed system. Months later, Lamb-Weston learned that the blade contractor was working on a project for McCain and had him sign a confidentiality agreement. At that time, Lamb-Weston also sent a letter to McCain, citing concerns that McCain may have been misappropriating its trade secrets. McCain entered into an exclusivity agreement with the contractor sometime later and, as a consequence, received information from the contractor concerning the blade. McCain is said to have developed a working prototype of the system. As one may guess, Lamb-Weston filed suit, claiming its trade secrets had been misappropriated. As a result of the proceedings, McCain was enjoined from using the information for a period of eight months. The injunction included world-wide restrictions. McCain appealed.

One of the issues presented on appeal was whether or not the court abused its discretion in granting a world-wide injunction. A question was raised as to the appropriateness of the relatively long term of the injunction. The U.S. Court of Appeals for the Ninth Circuit heard the case.

In its deliberations, the court noted that Oregon law requires that, for a misappropriation of a trade secret to have occurred, one must prove that the information was valuable, that there was a confidential relationship between the owner of the secret and the person who disclosed it, and that the key design features of the system in dispute were the creative product of the person claiming damages.

It was noted that circumstantial evidence led to the conclusion that, despite assurances from the contractor to maintain confidentiality, it was apparent that such was unlikely. Simultaneously developing similar products for two competitors without using knowledge gleaned in one effort for the other is a difficult, if not impossible, challenge. The fact that the contractor kept both firms' prototype products in the same work room suggested to the court that he was using the same information to develop both products.

As far as secrecy is concerned, the patent application was a confidential document. When Lamb-Weston became concerned about the climate of confidentiality in the workplace of the contractor, it had him enter into a confidentiality agreement. The firm was concerned about its secrets and took steps to maintain them.

Finally, as far as the issues of the length of time and the world-wide restriction encompassed in the injunction, the court found that both were supported by the evidence. Lamb-Weston was an international firm doing business in several countries. Although it arguably was not present in all or even many countries, it was making efforts to further develop its international presence and viewed the new curlicue system as essential in such an effort. The length of the injunction was an issue as well. The court noted that injunctions are intended to protect trade secrets and eliminate any unfair head start that may have accrued from a misappropriation. Because the development of the blade was an involved, time-consuming effort, the length of the injunction was seen as reasonable. The court of appeals affirmed the injunction as issued by the lower court.

SUMMARY OF CONCEPTS

1. Information must be secret to qualify as a protectable secret.
2. Information must not be readily knowable to qualify as a protectable secret.
3. Public utilities and certain other statutorily regulated firms are subject to public records law.
4. Federal purchasing or acquisition laws may assist in maintaining secrecy.
5. Surplus documents need to be destroyed, files locked, and access restricted.
6. Reasonable efforts to maintain secrecy are expected, given the circumstances.
7. Existing employees can be bound to restrictive covenants, because courts have determined that the promise of continued employment is sufficient consideration to bind the parties.
8. Public disclosure of information results in a loss of its secrecy.
9. Injunctions can serve to eliminate an unfair head start achieved via a trade secrets misappropriation.
10. The UTSA does not preclude utilities and certain other firms operating under regulatory guidelines from filing reports aimed at securing the public health or good.

APPENDIX: CITATIONS AND MANAGEMENT IMPLICATIONS

Sheets v. Yamaha Motors Corporation, U.S.A. 849 F.2d 179 (5th Cir. 1988) — Secrecy must be maintained. Public display of a secret negates the secret.

Razorback Oil Tools International, Inc. v. Taylor Oil Tools Company 626 So.2d 28 (La.App. 1 Cir. 1993) — Secrets voluntarily surrendered, even through a sale of assets, may result in a loss of trade secret status for the information.

Courtesy Temporary Service, Inc. v. Camacho et al. 272 Cal.Rptr. 352 (Cal.App. 2 Dist. 1989) — The time, labor, expense, and ingenuity involved in developing a customer list may qualify such as a trade secret under the UTSA.

Abba Rubber Company v. Seaquist et al. 286 Cal.Rptr. 518 (Cal.App. 4 Dist. 1991) — A customer list for which value is shown to exist and for which reasonable measures have been taken to insure secrecy may qualify as a protectable secret. California's statute differs and may be perceived differently from the UTSA as adopted by other states.

IMI-Tech v. Gagliani et al. 691 F.Supp. 214 (S.D.Cal. 1986) — In California, even though one may be able to ascertain a secret, the fact that no one has ascertained the secret may result in garnering UTSA protection for the secret.

Gordon Employment, Inc. v. Jewell 356 N.W.2d 738 (Minn.App. 1984) — Restrict access to secrets. Secret information needs to be protected. Reasonable steps need to be taken to provide for the continued secrecy of one's trade secrets.

Acuson Corporation v. Aloka Company, LTD. 257 Cal.Rptr. 368 (Cal.App. 6 Dist. 1989) — Reverse engineering of secrets is not forbidden by the UTSA. Items containing secrets and sold or released to the public may result in a loss of secrets and legal protection.

Haan Crafts Corporation v. Craft Masters, Inc. 683 F.Supp. 1234 (N.D.Ind. 1988) — Items released to the public domain may be freely copied unless protected by trademark, patent, or copyright laws. Reverse engineering performed legally would negate secrecy.

Wright Chemical Corporation v. Johnson et al. 563 F.Supp. 501 (1983) — In situations in which reverse engineering can reveal trade secrets, trade secrets no longer exist.

Vault Corporation v. Quaid Software Limited 655 F.Supp. 750 (E.D.La. 1987) — Reverse engineering computer software to reveal secrets may lead to a discovery of trade secrets. Such use of secrets cannot violate copyright law if such is applicable. Only those whose rights have been infringed can claim infringement.

Sheets v. Yamaha Motors Corporation, U.S.A. 849 F.2d 179 (5th Cir. 1988) — Publicly displaying secrets negates the secrecy and results in a loss of UTSA protection.

Rockwell Graphic System, Inc. v. Dev Industries et al. 730 F.Supp. 171 (N.D.Ill. 1990) — Superficial controls will not secure secrets. Reasonable steps must be taken to maintain secrecy. Secure secrets at all times.

Insurance Associates Corporation v. Hansen et al. 723 P.2d 190 (Idaho App. 1986) — The promise of continued employment can be sufficient to bind an employee to an agreement, even after employment has commenced.

Secure Services Technology, Inc. v. Time and Space Processing, Inc. 722 F.Supp. 1354 (E.D.Va. 1989) — An atmosphere of confidentiality is a must. When dealing with the defense department, vouchers can assist in maintaining secrecy by noting the existence of confidential information and the expectation that confidentiality is to be maintained.

Indianapolis Convention & Visitors Association, Inc., v. Indianapolis Newspapers, Inc. 577 N.E.2d 208 (Ind. 1991) — Public agencies and quasi-public agencies are subject to open records law.

Northern States Power Company v. North Dakota Public Service Commission 502 N.W.2d 240 (N.D. 1993) — Price and volume data can constitute a trade secret. However, there is a legitimate public interest in required filings by utilities in which such information is revealed. Power companies are subject to open records laws relative to such data.

State of Alaska, Department of Natural Resources v. Artic Slope Regional Corporation et al. 834 P.2d 134 (Alaska 1991) — Well drilling data constitutes a trade secret. However, the state's reporting of such data pursuant to state law does not constitute an illegal taking of private property.

Avtec Systems Incorporated v. Peiffer et al. 21 F.3d 568 (4th Cir. 1994) — A nonexclusive license to use a program that is controlled by another who can sell or give away the secret at will does little to prove that the license owner has an interest in a protectable trade secret.

Lamb-Weston, Inc., v. McCain Foods, LTD. 941 F.2d 970 (9th Cir. 1991) — Confidentiality agreements can aid in establishing a climate of confidentiality. Injunctions can ensue to eliminate any head start one may receive via a misappropriation.

7

Developing a Plan of Action

Increasingly, executives are finding they are gatekeepers of valuable information for which they must plan to provide security. As relationships between firms lead to increasingly interdependent efforts on which the success of all depends, executives need to direct their efforts at maintaining their firm's competitive stance by maintaining the proprietary nature of their valuable secrets. Executives must take a proactive position with respect to trade secrets protection. As has been seen in numerous cases already presented, trade secrets can be lost quickly when inadequate planning or implementation procedures are followed. As seen, too, trade secrets can be lost through accident. It is imperative that, as new paradigms of corporate interrelationships appear, executives are cognizant of both the benefits such paradigms promise and the risks they pose to trade secrets and plan accordingly.

In recent years, a trend has developed that results in firms seeking out a minimum number of reliable sources of products, components, or services and relying on these few providers to service the needs of the contracting firm. Such contracts have at their core a "partnering" agreement, in which the parties work closely with one another to assure that the goals of each are accomplished. Part of the success Japanese firms have attained during the past 30 years is credited to its practice of *keiretsu*. *Keiretsu* encourages close, cooperative ties between firms, as found in partnering agreements. Japanese corporate culture encourages the reliance on only a few suppliers who are capable and willing to supply the necessary product or service at a quality level consistent with the buyer's objectives. In the United States, just-in-time partnering philosophy embodies the close working relationship for which the Japanese are known. Partnering agreements between buyers and sellers are taking many industries by storm, with no one wanting to be left out of the potential benefits that are said to accrue from such close working relationships. Partnering agreements raise many issues of concern to executives. One of these, and one that deserves close attention, is the necessity to provide adequate protection for trade secrets.

The trade secrets security issue arises in a partnering association because vendors receive more exposure to the internal operations of a buyer, have improved access to the buyer's processes, and generally possess a level of intimacy with the buying organization that heretofore has not been seen in corporate culture. Indeed, it is no longer an unheard-of practice for buyers to offer to provide office space and other on-site support to their critical suppliers in order to improve inventory flow and maintain delivery. Increasingly, as a result, executives are finding they are becoming guardians of valuable information that flows to and through the organization — information that is at risk. It is the need to adequately protect this flow of information, proprietary, valuable information, that presents a challenge to executives to provide for the security of trade secrets while providing for the continued success of their competitive efforts.

Executives involved in partnering agreements expose trade secrets and make them vulnerable to discovery by others in a variety of ways. Knowledge of the materials going into a product or process potentially gives a partnering associate insights into processes and material content that may not be available to the casual or even determined observer who lacks such close knowledge. On-site access by suppliers poses risks that did not necessarily exist prior to the concept of partnering. Despite these and other potential exposure risks, benefits to both parties in some partnering arrangements are said to accrue and obviously are seen as outweighing the risks to trade secrets security.

Partnering agreements can and often do result in performance improvements and increased profits by firms so obligated to contractual partners. Just-in-time production and other inventory systems can be effectuated, with cost savings and improved profitability as a result of improvements associated with such inventory control systems. Contract negotiating and supplier search costs are reduced when the number of contracts is reduced, as is the necessity to seek additional sources, once a reliable source is on board. Many firms have reported results with their partnering agreements similar to those of Xerox, which O'Neal reports has improved its performance as a result of its concurrent engineering–early supplier involvement program. In summary, partnering agreements offer an improved, symbiotic relationship between suppliers and buyers.

Still, despite their many undisputed benefits, partnering arrangements necessitate an exchange of information that may be considered secret by one or both of the parties to the agreement. New product plans, proprietary processes, market research results, customer requirements, and other proprietary information often are exchanged by the partners as a consequence of the agreement. Such information usually is not intended for dissemination or use beyond the boundaries of the agreement. It is this disclosure and sharing of trade secrets through partnering agreements and other close contractual arrangements that demands careful consideration and planning to assure the continued protection of the information and prevent its disclosure to others.

Executives need to give careful consideration to provide for the protection of valuable secrets that may be compromised during the negotiation process, during the life of an agreement stipulating the provisions of the partnering arrangement, and for a period of time after such an agreement expires. Misappropriations of trade secrets can be very costly to firms that lose the competitive advantage previously afforded them by virtue of their proprietary secrets. For instance, General Electric's proprietary formula for making high quality, synthetic diamonds was reported stolen in 1990. The estimated value of the formula was reported to be at least $5 million. Potentially proprietary information, including research findings, new product plans, process secrets, new market entry plans, location analyses, and other types of valuable information, serves as the basis for successful competitive efforts; therefore, it needs to be protected. Providing for the protection of secrets in both domestic and international transactions not only is a good management practice but also may be legally necessary in certain circumstances, given the provisions of the Export Administration Act. The Export Administration Act is a federal law that concerns restrictions on certain goods used in international trade. Again, a firm desiring to protect its secrets needs competent legal counsel. It is important to recognize that consideration needs to be given to providing adequate security when negotiating partnering arrangements. Indeed, in the supplier selection and evaluation process, security considerations should play an important role if one expects to continue to receive the benefits of owning valuable trade secrets.

Numerous studies of partnering arrangements and their impact on competitiveness lead to an interesting conclusion. Among the major factors considered when buyers search out and assess potential suppliers are the quality of delivered products or services rendered, prices of the products or services, the ability of the supplier to provide the kinds of after-the-sale service (for example, maintenance, quick delivery) needed by the buyer, and, to a lesser extent, flexibility in serving the needs of the buyer. Without exception, in listing the factors found to impact decisions leading to partnering arrangements, it is interesting that an assessment of a supplier's climate of confidentiality and its potential impact on a firm's trade secrets do not appear to make anyone's list of important considerations.

Executives considering entering partnering agreements with suppliers need to evaluate the ability of suppliers to serve their needs and contribute to their operations. Trust as a valuation needs to be among the factors used in such an assessment. Information concerning the place of ethics in a supplier's business practices and references from knowledgeable individuals or organizations should be sought and used in the evaluation process. Owners of trade secrets that may be compromised need to initiate discussions about steps the supplier intends to take to provide for the protection of the secrets. Does the potential partner require nondisclosure, noncompetition agreements of its employees? Would it be willing to include a provision in such agreements that precludes them from disclosing or competing with the potential partner? Considering that valuable information is at stake, does the supplier intend to take steps that are reasonable given the circumstances to protect the information? What steps, specifically, will be taken to maintain security of the secrets? Will the partner to whom secrets will be entrusted allow an audit of these steps so as to insure their completion? Executives entering into such agreements who are responsible for their firms' secrets need to assess the climate of confidentiality in place at the supplier's operating site. Establishing that a potential partner is trustworthy, honest, and conscientious about security is wise. With the increased presence of outsiders in one's operations as a result of a partnering agreement and the resulting access to one's trade secrets, a candid and thorough assessment of trustworthiness of a partner and that partner's climate of confidentiality is essential to protect one's secret.

Contracts covering the parameters of partnering arrangements need to be developed that detail protection and confidentiality expectations and competitive restrictions on all of the parties involved. Another potentially advantageous provision to include in such agreements is how disputes between the parties would be approached and resolved. Hopefully, the contract would require arbitration or some other binding effort short of having to resort to the courts for resolution of a disagreement. Agreements should detail nondisclosure and noncompetition expectations. It would be preferable that the partner also be required to have its employees enter into comparable agreements that dictate a similar level of restraint. The agreement should dictate a reasonable period after the termination of the partnering agreement during which the partner and its employees still would be expected to maintain confidentiality and a noncompetitive mode. Additionally, it is the responsibility of the trade secrets owner to assess compliance with the contract provisions and assure that the partner is adhering to all provisions regarding maintenance of secrets as specified in the contract. Although the Uniform Trade Secrets Act may not be law in all jurisdictions, its scope and its intent can help executives seeking to be involved in partnering agreements develop a plan of action that will acknowledge and provide for the protection of trade secrets.

The idea of having a potential partner's employees sign a nondisclosure, noncompetition agreement is important. It is especially important to recognize that such agreements must discern specifically an employee's intent not to use or disclose trade secrets belonging to the originating partner, usually the buying firm, or enter into competition with the originating partner during the term of the agreement or for a reasonable period after its expiration. A case that originated in Illinois in which this issue played an important role was the case of *Composite Marine Propellers, Inc. v. Van Der Woude et al.*, which was heard on appeal by the United States Court of Appeals for the Seventh Circuit.

Composite Marine Propellers was known for the quality of its boat propellers, which were made from a composite plastic-based material. The propellers were produced via an allegedly secret process that formed the composite material. The resulting propellers possessed central hubs made of metal. The company's principal supplier had signed a contract that included noncompetition, nondisclosure, and nonuse provisions relative to Composite's trade secrets. The agreement also specified that the supplier would obtain comparable promises in the form of express agreements from its employees.

As has been seen in many cases alleging trade secrets misappropriation, the resignation, departure, and subsequent competitive efforts of a few employees led to charges being filed alleging damages. In this case, the supplier's former employees established their own firm to produce plastic propellers. A major difference in the propellers of the upstart firm and those of Composite was that the new firm's product did not contain the central metal hub evident in Composite's products. Composite Marine sued the former employees of the new firm, claiming trade secrets infringement. Among the trade secrets that Composite charged had been misappropriated were marketing plans and strategies, the use of gas counter back pressure in the molding process, material characteristics, mold cooling methodology, and various test data.

Among the items of interest that came to light during the case was the fact that the supplier had failed to have its employees agree to noncompetition covenants. In addition, Composite Marine did not conduct an audit or other assessment of the steps that the supplier had taken in response to its agreement to protect Composite's trade secrets. Van Der Woude, a principal in the new firm and a defendant in this case, obtained a patent covering the production of an all-plastic propeller. Van Der Woude reportedly had filed a separate suit against Composite Marine, claiming it infringed on his patent. The plaintiff claims that the supplier's employees were bound by common-law principles of fiduciary duty and unfair competition not to enter into competition against it and were using its trade secrets in producing their patented propeller. Finally, Composite Marine claimed that the former employees of its supplier should be prohibited from entering into competition with it because of the existence of the agreement between Composite Marine and its supplier, which expressly forbid competition on the part of the supplier.

The court of appeals considered the question of trade secrets infringement. It concluded that there was no evidence that the defendants had used any of Composite's trade secrets. As the court noted, to qualify as a trade secret, information must be secret, not be generally known or readily ascertainable, and be subject to efforts that are reasonable under the circumstances to maintain secrecy. To find that a misappropriation occurred, there would have to be evidence that the secrets had been acquired in an unauthorized manner and were being used by individuals in their commercial pursuits.

Although certain information, such as the optimum flexibility properties to embody in the propellers, was found to be a trade secret of Composite, there was no evidence presented to show that the flex information had been misappropriated. Indeed, it was established that a different flexibility factor had been utilized in the design of the competing propellers, as expressly was stated in the Van Der Woude patent application. The use of a different flexibility factor precluded a misappropriation of the specific flexibility factor claimed by Composite as its secret.

The charge that secrets relative to Composite's marketing plans had been misappropriated also were found lacking. Specifically, a strategic decision by a firm to enter a market, any market, is not necessarily an indication that trade secrets have been misappropriated. Such a move may be, and perhaps often is, a recognition that a particular market is perceived as holding significant commercial promise. The defendants' actions to enter the marine propeller market, given their experience in the industry, should not be surprising. The court found that the firm's market entry did not equate with the misappropriation of a trade secret. Potentially furthering the court's finding that the market knowledge did not qualify as a trade secret was testimony from a principal of Composite, who testified that he had discussions concerning channels of distribution relative to the propeller market with numerous individuals in the industry. Therefore, one would be correct in concluding that information recognizing opportunities in the market and relative to distribution channels did not qualify as a protectable trade secret.

The charge of misappropriation of secrets relative to the use of gas counter back pressure in the molding process also was found lacking by the court. Testimony indicated that the use of gas counter back pressure in the molding process was a well-known procedure in the industry. Its use by Composite had been based on technology-sharing demonstrations of the process by another firm in the industry. There was no secret attached to the use of gas counter back pressure to improve the finish of the final product. Other firms had been using the technique for years. Without a secret, there could be no misappropriation. The finding that the use of gas counter back pressure in the molding process was not a trade secret and, thus, could not be misappropriated is not surprising, given the testimony.

The materials-related charge of misappropriation likewise was found lacking in substance. The two firms used different types of plastic in the formulations of their products. Even when the fiber materials embodied within the plastic composites were found to be similar, their proportions were not comparable. The court found that there had been a total failure of proof relative to claims related to misappropriations of Composite's secrets as found in its composite formula.

Composite's remaining alleged secrets were, likewise, found not to have existed or have been infringed upon. In what is undoubtedly a rare occurrence, the court of appeals reversed a trial jury's finding. At the trial, the jury found that Composite had been the victim of a trade secrets misappropriation and, as a result, had incurred damages. As determined by the higher court, either Composite's alleged secrets did not exist or, in the instance in which the secret was shown to exist, the plaintiff firm had failed to prove a misappropriation had occurred.

Finally, and perhaps most importantly to those considering entering partnering arrangements, the court found that the defendants were within their rights to enter into competition with Composite. The defendants did not engage in unfair competition or violate any fiduciary duties owed to

Composite. They had not misappropriated trade secrets of the plaintiff. The contract that prohibited the supplier from entering into a competitive situation with Composite did not bind the supplier's employees. The supplier entered into the contract with Composite and, therefore, was precluded from competing in the market. Its employees, though, given the fact that they had not entered into similar agreements with Composite, were free to enter the market.

In preparing a plan of action with the aim of protecting trade secrets, several questions need to be addressed. Who will have access to the information, and under what circumstances will access be provided? Are nondisclosure covenants in place that provide for adequate protection? Is the information kept in locked areas? Is it marked "confidential"? Are visitors prohibited from entering areas where secrets may be compromised? These and other security concerns need to be addressed in plans aimed at providing adequate security for secrets.

The need to provide for reasonable security and the factors that such might entail were evident in *Surgidev Corporation v. Eye Technology, Inc.* Surgidev Corporation was a California based manufacturer of intraocular lenses. The company's target market consisted of a specialized group of ophthalmologists who were high volume purchasers and users of intraocular lenses. A list of such medical providers was considered to be a trade secret of Surgidev. Eye Technology, Inc., was a competitive firm whose principals primarily were former employees of Surgidev. At trial in which charges of misappropriation of trade secrets was alleged, the court found for Surgidev and enjoined the defendant from engaging in certain competitive business operations for a period of 15 months.

The trial court's finding apparently focused on testimony of witnesses who testified that the identities of high volume users of intraocular lenses, as contained in the disputed customer list, were not generally known in the industry and that sufficient effort was needed to develop such a list. In addition, the court found that the defendant intended to use the customer list to its competitive advantage. Because of the finding of apparent intent by the defendant to use the list to its advantage, the court rejected the argument that the list had no value. An intent to use the list of doctors indicated to the court that the list did hold competitive value.

Just as important to the court's determination that the customer list was a protectable trade secret were the specific actions Surgidev had taken to protect its secrets. The list was kept in a locked file in a secured area. Employees were required to sign nondisclosure, noncompetition covenants. Customer information was released to employees only on a need to know basis and, after authorized use, was resecured. Finally, the firm had strict policies regulating visitor access to its office areas. Such efforts to secure the information were deemed to be reasonable, given the circumstances.

The customer list had value. The customer list was secret. Reasonable steps to maintain the secrecy of the information on the list had been implemented and monitored for compliance. In short, the information was a protectable trade secret. The United States Court of Appeals for the Eighth Circuit upheld the order of the lower court enjoining the defendants from pursuing business with high volume intraocular lens users for a period of 15 months, or otherwise making use of Surgidev's trade secrets.

In *Rockwell Graphic System, Inc. v. Dev Industries et al.*, discussed at length in an earlier chapter, it was noted that Rockwell regularly threw away surplus or unneeded documents that contained its trade secrets. Perhaps surprising to some is the fact that one's trash is not a secure haven. If one has unneeded copies of secret documents, they should be destroyed, not thrown away.

In any environment in which trade secrets are utilized and their protection desired, it must be realized that reasonable steps need to be taken to maintain their secrecy. The information needs to be locked away or otherwise secured when not in use. Locking the information in locked file cabinets is a start. Deciding who will have access to the information and under what circumstances are necessary steps in a protection plan. As for the disposition of documents that are no longer needed, policy expectations should center on the destruction of the information. In concert with legal counsel, nondisclosure, noncompete agreements need to be developed that are reasonable and legal as to time and place.

SUMMARY OF CONCEPTS

1. Reasonable steps need to be taken to maintain secrecy.
2. Restrict secrets' availability or access to those who have a need to know.
3. Destroy surplus copies of documents.
4. Provide physical security for the secrets.
5. Use restrictive covenants.
6. Restrictive covenants are recommended for all parties who have access to the secrets.
7. Provide for an opportunity to insure that steps are being followed by periodically conducting a trade secrets audit.

APPENDIX: CITATIONS AND
MANAGEMENT IMPLICATIONS

Composite Marine Propellers, Inc. v. Van Der Woude et al. 962 F.2d 1263 (7th Cir. 1992) — Noncompetition covenants binding suppliers from competing with buyers do not bind or obligate the employees of suppliers not to compete.

Surgidev Corporation v. Eye Technology, Inc. 828 F.2d 452 (8th Cir. 1987) — Reasonable steps under the circumstances need to be taken to maintain secrecy. Restricting access, providing physical security in locked files, and the use of employee covenants prohibiting disclosure all can lead to the conclusion that information is a trade secret. Such efforts need to be a part of strategic planning.

Rockwell Graphic System, Inc. v. Dev Industries et al. 730 F.Supp. 171 (N.D.Ill 1990) — Destroy copies of documents containing trade secrets. Do not throw them away.

8

Legal Avenues and Alternatives

By now, if one thing is not clear, it needs to be made clear here. Trade secrets protection efforts involve an area of the law — an area of the law that, with the implementation of the Uniform Trade Secrets Act (UTSA) is becoming increasingly easier to understand, given the specificity of the act and the cases that have ensued, an area of the law for which you will need competent legal advice.

When choosing an attorney to advise management on trade secrets protection efforts, one needs to find an attorney that is experienced in commercial law. Choosing a divorce specialist is not sound practice unless one is contemplating a divorce. Because the concept of trade secrets is embodied in commercial law, a competent individual with experience in that area of law is desired. Firms that currently do not have a competent legal advisor have three logical avenues to pursue in search of such counsel.

First, executives of firms that currently do not have legal counsel may check with other noncompeting firms in the area for information on their experience with their outside attorneys and recommendations pursuant to their experience. Firsthand knowledge and experience can go a long way to make a case as to one's qualifications and experience with commercial law. In checking with other executives, inquire as to the quality of service provided by the attorney and as to what types of problems their attorneys were especially adept at handling. Make it clear that an attorney with commercial law experience is desired.

Second, a search for attorneys with commercial law experience can be conducted at many libraries. Law libraries, most university libraries, and many public libraries carry the *Martindale-Hubbell Law Directory* in the reference section. The directory geographically lists the names of most attorneys practicing in the United States. Each attorney's reported area of specialty is listed, along with any state-issued certification in a number of specialty areas. The *Martindale-Hubbell Law Directory* can be a good source of information on attorneys.

Finally, an executive desiring the services of an attorney with experience in commercial law usually can call the bar association, headquartered in their state's capital. Most bar associations operate attorney referral services, which will provide the names and contact information for attorneys fitting an explicit request parameter. Again, attorneys with commercial law experience, specifically, trade secrets experience, would be preferable. The bar can help executives by directing them to such an attorney.

When choosing an attorney, one should narrow down choices and make an appointment to interview the attorney. One should choose an attorney who makes one feel comfortable. The attorney should appear knowledgeable and answer reasonable questions of the interviewer. At such an interview, the attorney preferably would speak in the language of the layman, not undecipherable legalese. If the attorney does not speak in language that the executive can understand or cannot answer basic questions about dealing with trade secrets, the executive should seek another candidate. An executive usually does not want an attorney who speaks about legal theories in a foreign language. One needs an attorney who is knowledgeable about such matters, who can put that knowledge to practical use, and who can do so in a manner that is understandable by the client.

In addition to knowledge of trade secrets law, an attorney who is knowledgeable about contract law, unfair trade practice acts, employment law, the Freedom of Information Act, and other laws that may be relevant to one's specific business can offer the firm an even better and more comprehensive service. Establishing a good relationship with one's attorney is a good business practice. Such a relationship, coupled with an understanding of one's business and trade secrets laws, will aid in one's planning to develop effective trade secrets protection efforts.

Having an attorney in on the planning process from the beginning is paramount in one's efforts to adequately protect one's secrets. It is cheap assurance that the firm will be following both a practical and a legal course of action aimed at providing reasonable security. Once the planning process identifies trade secrets and plans are instituted to protect the secrets, the attorney can help make sure that the firm continues to follow the intent and well as the specifics of the law.

It cannot be emphasized enough that the UTSA is a state law, a uniform state law but a state law nonetheless. Therefore, there are minor differences in some of the states' versions. Additionally, laws that often enter into discussions revolving around trade secrets issues often are state laws and vary widely as to their specifics. Chief among these would be unfair trade practice acts, the specifics and impacts of which vary among the states. Because of changes in laws over time, it is important that a firm seeking protection of its trade secrets pursue competent legal advice in the geographic area or areas in which it operates.

Finally, the cases included in this book are typical cases as pursued under the provisions of the UTSA and are presented for explanatory purposes. They do not represent all of the cases or all of the potential circumstances under which a claim for trade secrets misappropriation may occur. For that reason, they and the plan in this book need to be used as a foundation for an understanding of the act, its scope, and its impact. Such an understanding should be used as the basis for discussions with one's legal counsel and present a basis for management to begin its efforts to adequately protect its secrets. The analyses of the cases presented in this book and the action plan as recommended should not be construed as legal advice. That is the role one's attorney plays, and, therefore, the necessity for competent legal counsel in preparations centering around protecting one's trade secrets cannot be overstated.

As may be gleaned from the inclusion of the case of *McMahan Securities Company, L.P. v. Forum Capital Markets, L.P. et al.* in this book, when possible, arbitration of disputes has its advantages. As the court noted in *Abba Rubber Company v. Seaquist et al.*, "litigation is extraordinarily expensive. That is especially true in commercial litigation such as this, in which two businesses are fighting over the right to sell to a particular customer base amid allegations of misappropriation of trade secrets." The costs associated with a trade secrets case can be exorbitantly high for all parties. Remember, for a plaintiff to recover attorney fees, the UTSA specifies that a willful and malicious misappropriation must have occurred. Although misappropriations sometimes are easy to prove, proving that a misappropriation was willful and malicious is more difficult.

Therefore, in some circumstances, it is more prudent to provide for another avenue for dispute resolution. Partnering agreements in particular should include specific provisions detailing dispute resolution. Such a provision wisely would cover all disputes arising during the course of the partnering contract, not just trade secrets disputes. Partnering agreements can be effective when the operations of the two parties do not become so burdensome as to be negatively impacted. Trying to settle each and every partnering dispute in a courtroom undoubtedly would remove any benefits potentially accruing from a partnering arrangement. In partnering agreements, arbitration is a faster, cheaper method of dispute resolution than the courtroom alternative. Also, in recent years, professional arbitrators have become attuned increasingly to the law and its interpretation. Arbitration of disputes should be provided for in a partnering contract.

The probability of resolving every trade secrets dispute through arbitration is not high. It does not require much thought to realize that, when former employees are involved in a dispute, there may be more difficulty in settling trade secrets disputes through arbitration than may be found in an explicit agreement stipulating such an effort between partners. Still, it does not mean it cannot be done. Arbitration of trade secrets disputes offers benefits that parties to such disputes need to consider.

A final alternative to actually going to court is settling a case prior to the court date. Although this may not be of interest to one or both parties, this is often a cheaper method and, if settled in a just manner, may prove more advantageous to both parties than pursuing the action in court. Advice from legal counsel on both sides of the dispute can aid their clients in a settlement resolution — another reason that attorneys who are familiar with trade secrets law need to be involved in one's protection efforts. Knowledgeable advice as to when or when not to settle is needed in such circumstances.

Finally, the issues revolving around trade secrets are legal issues, but it is not the intent of this book to prepare one to go to court. Taking a case to court will consume much time, interfere with ongoing operations, be costly, and is nerve wracking. If court can be avoided and one's secrets maintained, significant benefits to the owner of a secret will ensue. The intent of the protection plan discussed is to emphasize that, if one develops a climate of confidentiality, protects one's secrets, and takes other steps that are reasonable to maintain secrecy, one may not be as likely to have to pursue rights in court. Hopefully, one's secrets will be secure.

SUMMARY OF CONCEPTS

1. As in any situation involving the law, obtain legal counsel from the start.

2. In choosing an attorney, choose one with commercial law expertise.

3. Pursuing a court case involving trade secrets disputes can be costly.

4. There are alternatives, foremost of which is arbitration, which may be available to an executive for dispute resolution.

APPENDIX: CITATIONS AND MANAGEMENT IMPLICATIONS

McMahan Securities Company, L.P. v. Forum Capital Markets, L.P. et al. 35 F.3d 82 (2nd Cir. 1994) — Arbitration clauses can and will be enforced. Arbitration may reduce costs associated with disputes arising from trade secrets disputes.

Abba Rubber Company, v. Seaquist et al. 286 Cal.Rptr. 518 (Cal.App. 4 Dist. 1991) — Litigation of trade secrets disputes can be extraordinarily expensive.

9

Summary of Trade Secrets Protection under the Uniform Trade Secrets Act

Trade secrets are composed of information that is secret, valuable, and subject to efforts deemed reasonable under the circumstances to maintain its secrecy. Business executives sometimes can choose between trade secrets statutes and other proprietary property laws such as patent laws in deciding how best to protect their valuable information from which they derive a competitive advantage.

Trade secrets laws are state laws. Therefore, they historically varied in their scope and specifics among the states. Trying to understand the many intricacies involved among the various acts was a difficult task at best. For firms operating in more than one state, working in an environment with a variety of laws was a daunting challenge. However, a new law, the Uniform Trade Secrets Act (UTSA) promises to replace the hodgepodge of states' laws and replace it with one comprehensive and specific act. The UTSA offers consistent protection of trade secrets to those operating in jurisdictions that have adopted the act. So far, 40 states and the District of Columbia have adopted the act.

In looking at the UTSA and the cases that have already ensued under its auspices, one is struck by the simplicity of the act and its comprehensive coverage of concerns of secrets owners. The act is a clear, simple, power-ful tool in the management arsenal. Still, despite its power, the real management benefit to accrue from an understanding of the UTSA lies in its ability to alert management to the necessity of taking proactive steps to protect one's secrets. It is the recognition that trade secrets are valuable, secret information that require reasonable efforts to maintain their secrecy that serves as a lesson to executives. Executives need to take an organized approach to providing for the protection of their secrets.

Executives need to take proactive steps in order to provide adequately for the protection of secrets with which they are entrusted. First among these steps should be a listing of the steps and procedures that will be implemented to insure compliance. Developing the list will help to assure their completion, because it can serve as a checklist and audit record. Then, assuming that the information for which the secrecy is desired has been delineated, steps to secure the information will need to be implemented. Remember, the UTSA expects that steps that are reasonable given the circumstances will be taken to maintain secrecy. Efforts that may be deemed reasonable in one work environment may not be in another. The procedural steps mentioned here may not be applicable or necessary in every work environment. Which of these procedures or, perhaps, others that need to be implemented must be decided by an executive and his or her legal counsel, based on the circumstances in which they operate.

Marking the information as "confidential" is a start. That means physically stamping the folders, diagrams, blueprints, and other physical forms of the secret as being confidential and not for disclosure or use. If the information is stored in electronic files, it is a good idea that an opening screen display a confidentiality message when an individual accesses the file. Simple marking of the information as secret and not for disclosure or use is an easy step and one that is cheap.

The information needs to be locked up or otherwise secured when not in use. Locking the information in locked file cabinets is a start. If the information is very valuable, securing it in a safe may not be inappropriate. If the information is in the form of blueprints, listings, or other documents that are checked out of a "control" room, procedures need to be in place to insure that the information is returned and resecured. If the information of concern is stored in an electronic medium, specific computer security steps, such as password protection, need to be considered. If the computer files are accessible from offsite, access security may require a higher level of security than if offsite access is not provided. The areas in which the secrets are used and stored should be restricted from visitor access.

Deciding who will have access to the information and under what circumstances is a necessary step in a protection plan. A situation in which almost anyone can view or learn the secret usually will not suffice as an effort deemed reasonable under the circumstances to maintain secrecy. In many firms, it is not necessary that everyone have access to the secrets. It is a good posture to decide who can have access, when they can have access, and under what circumstances. Limiting access can serve to limit secrets' disclosure risks.

As for the disposition of documents that are no longer needed, policy expectations should center on the destruction of the information. Employees should not throw the information in the trash. One does not throw away "valuable" secrets. Old or surplus copies of the documents should be shredded, burned, or otherwise destroyed. If the information is on computer disk or tape, it should be permanently degaussed or burned. If the shredded information is of high value, consider the use of a cross-shredder or multiple-pass shredder, which turns a document into confetti, not easily rejoined strips. Cross shredding? Burning? Will a competitor really seek out one's trash for secrets it might contain? Is the total destruction of documents containing trade secrets really necessary? Again, it depends on the circumstances.

If one's trade secrets are really valuable, the circumstances may dictate such an effort. As for the potential that one's trash may pose a security risk, there have been several cases in which computer hackers reportedly obtained, in trash cans situated outside of major firms, passwords and other information from documents and notes that allowed them access into computer systems. Wendy Zellner and Bruce Hager (1991) reported that employees of the cosmetics giant Mary Kay Corporation caught private detectives rummaging through its trash dumpster. The detectives, purportedly, were under contract to an equally famous competitor, Avon Products, Inc. Most of the documents recovered by the detectives were shredded, but this apparently did not deter them from taking the materials. Those around during the Iranian hostage situation several years back may remember the newsreels showing Iranian soldiers in the U.S. embassy painstakingly recompiling U.S. government secret documents that had been shredded shortly before the building was overrun. Destroying documents that are valuable is a good practice and reduces risks of disclosure.

In concert with legal counsel, nondisclosure, noncompete agreements need to be developed that are reasonable and legal as to time and place and, thus, enforceable. Employees should be required to sign the agreements, and yes, current employees can be bound to such an agreement, as are new hires. If working in a partnering agreement, one needs to have a contract stipulating nondisclosure, noncompete agreements. The contracting firm also should require the partner to have its employees sign similar agreements specifying they are bound from such actions to the partner, not just to their employer. Periodic reminders to employees as to the need to maintain secrecy may prove of value. Exit interviews with departing employees, reminding them of their obligations as stipulated in their employment agreement, are a good idea. Having the employee sign a statement attesting to the meeting and its content may also prove of value though, in circumstances surrounding some termination proceedings, understandably impossible to obtain.

Firms should consider periodic trade secrets audits. The right to audit security surrounding trade secrets should be stipulated in partnering agreements. Within a work environment, someone needs to be responsible for assuring that all procedures regarding the security of the secrets are being followed. In larger firms that have internal auditors, it can be argued that trade secrets auditing is as important as financial auditing. Internal auditors are responsible for the security of a firm's assets. It should be a part of their responsibility to assure the security of proprietary assets along with the other assets of the firm.

Finally, the UTSA offers protection for trade secrets. Astute executives will develop an understanding of the act and its scope, prepare plans in conjunction with their legal counsel to protect such secrets, and remain vigilant to the need to maintain their secrets.

The UTSA does not expect the impossible from executives. It expects that reasonable efforts will be expended to protect one's trade secrets. For those executives willing to take reasonable efforts to protect their proprietary trade information, the UTSA offers a welcome addition to the property rights already granted through trademark, copyright, and patent laws.

Selected Readings

Arnott, Nancy. 1994. "Don't Look Now." *Sales & Marketing Management Magazine*, December 1994, pp. 52–57.

Bleakley, Fred R. 1995. "Strange Bedfellows: Some Companies Let Suppliers Work On Site And Even Place Orders." *The Wall Street Journal*, January 13, 1995, pp. A1, A6.

Budden, Michael C. 1995. "Can You Keep A Secret?" *Business & Economic Review*, April/May/June 1995, pp. 24–26.

____. 1989. "Keep Your Practice Secrets Secret." *Dental Economics*, November 1989, pp. 35–37.

Budden, Michael C., Connie B. Budden, and Jerry L. Goodson. 1995. "Protecting Your Bank's Management and Marketing Secrets." *Marketing Update*, April 1995, pp. 1–4.

Budden, Michael C., Michael A. Jones, and Connie B. Budden. 1996. "Supplier Relationships and the Trade Secrets Dilemma." *International Journal of Purchasing and Materials Management*, Summer 1996, pp. 45–49.

Budden, Michael C., Robert C. Lake, and Samuel Lett. 1990. "Protecting Trade Secrets." *Management Accounting*, December 1990, pp. 45–47.

Budden, Michael C., Robert C. Lake, and John W. Yeargain. 1995. "Strategic Planning For Protection of Business Secrets Under the Uniform Trade Secrets Act." *Journal of Managerial Issues*, Fall 1995, pp. 343–57.

Carley, William M. 1995. "A Chip Comes In From The Cold: Tales of High-Tech Spying." *The Wall Street Journal*, January 19, 1995, pp. A1, A12.

Carter, Roy. 1989. "Careless Words Cost Business." *Accountancy* (England), March 1989, pp. 158–60.

Cunningham, Cara A. 1992. "Borland-Symantec Case Heats Up." *PC Week*, September 14, 1992, pp. 1, 11.

Doe, P. 1988. "Japan Starts Fighting For Its Own Patent Rights." *Electronic Business*, September 1, 1988, pp. 36–38.

Freedom of Information Act Guide & Privacy Act Overview. 1994. Washington, D.C.: U.S. Government Printing Office.

Gersh, Debra. 1993. "New FoIA Policy Directives Issued." *Editor & Publisher* 126 (1993): 18, 35.

Guida, Richard A. 1989. "The Costs of Free Information." *Public Interest*, Fall 1989, pp. 87–95.

Hanson, David. 1994. "Activist Groups Sue EPA Over Pesticide Formulas." *Chemical & Engineering News* 72 (1994): 6–7.

Haluch, Frank. 1992. "Are You Giving Away Trade Secrets?" *NAPMInsights*, September 1992, p. 25.

Ingrassia, Lawrence. 1990. "How Secret G.E. Recipe for Making Diamonds May Have Been Stolen." *The Wall Street Journal*, February 28, 1990, p. A1.

Jones, Arthur. 1992. "CI versus Spy." *Financial World*, April 28, 1992, pp. 62–64.

Lake, Robert C., Michael C. Budden, and Samuel Lett. 1991. "Trade Secrets Protection." *Internal Auditor*, August 1991, pp. 43–48.

Martindale-Hubbell Law Directory. New Providence, N.J.: Martindale-Hubbell, Inc.

Miller, Michael W. 1992. "IBM Sues To Silence Former Employee." *The Wall Street Journal*, July 15, 1992, p. B1.

"Mum's the Word." 1993. *Datamation*, February 1, 1993, p. 19.

Newton, Joseph Fort. 1939. *We Here Highly Resolve.* New York: Harper & Brothers Publishers.

O'Neal, Charles. 1993. "Concurrent Engineering with Early Supplier Involvement: A Cross Functional Challenge." *International Journal of Purchasing and Materials Management*, Spring 1993, pp. 3–9.

Plueddeman, Charles. 1995. "Secret Weapon." *Popular Mechanics*, April 1995, pp. 132, 135.

Reifenberg, Anne. 1995. "How Secret Formula For Coveted Slick 50 Fell Into Bad Hands." *The Wall Street Journal*, October 25, 1995, pp. A1, A9.

Simpson, Glenn R. 1995. "A '90s Espionage Tale Stars Software Rivals, E-Mail Spy." *The Wall Street Journal*, October 25, 1995, pp. B1, B4.

Taylor III, Alex. 1993. "VW's Rocky Road Ahead." *Fortune*, August 23, 1993, pp. 64–68.

Zellner, Wendy, and Bruce Hager. 1991 "Dumpster Raids? That's Not Very Ladylike, Avon." *Business Week*, April 1, 1991, p. 32.

Index of Legal Citations

Index

ABOUT THE AUTHOR

MICHAEL CRAIG BUDDEN is Professor of Marketing at Auburn University Montgomery, Montgomery, Alabama, with additional experience as a high-level university administrator. Author of more than 100 articles and scholarly publications, mostly on legal issues affecting business, he has served as consultant to a variety of banks, retailers, and professional associations.